THE
UNCOMMON QUILTER

THE
UNCOMMON QUILTER

Small Art Quilts Created with Paper, Plastic, Fiber, and Surface Design

JEANNE WILLIAMSON

POTTER
CRAFT

New York

In loving memory of Jordan Klaristenfeld and Earl Ostroff

Published in the United States by Potter Craft,
an imprint of the Crown Publishing Group,
a division of Random House, Inc., New York.
www.crownpublishing.com
www.pottercraft.com

POTTER CRAFT and CLARKSON N. POTTER are trademarks,
and POTTER and colophon are registered trademarks of Random House, Inc.

Library of Congress Cataloging-in-Publication Data
Williamson, Jeanne.
The uncommon quilter : small art quilts created with paper, plastic, fiber, and surface design/ by Jeanne Williamson.
p. cm.
Includes index.
ISBN-13: 978-0-307-38122-4 (trade pbk.)   1. Quilting.   2. Miniature quilts.   I. Title.
TT835.W5368 2007
746.46'041—dc22 2006034274

Printed in China

Design by : La Tricia Watford
Illustrations: Mike Gellatly
Quilt photography: David Caras
Author photograph: Joshua Touster
Chapter opener photography: Jeanne Williamson

1 3 5 7 9 10 8 6 4 2

Acknowledgments

I am thankful to many artists, friends, family, and professionals in my life for helping to bring this book to you.

For their help and expertise, I am very grateful to everyone with whom I worked at Potter Craft, especially Rosemary Ngo, Isa Loundon, Lauren Monchik, and La Tricia Watford.

Thanks to my agent, Sorche Fairbank, who worked incredibly hard to bring this book to life; to Barbara Bourassa, for editorial assistance and serenity; to Michael Gellatly, for his patience and talent for creating wonderful illustrations; to David Caras, for photographing all the 365 quilts I have created between 1999 and 2005; and to Joshua Touster, for his portrait photography.

This project would never have come to fruition without the love and support of Joshua Ostroff, Jonah Ostroff, Miryam Williamson, and Elaine Ostroff.

I am thankful for Danielle Dimston, who inspired me to be more experimental in my artwork. Thank you to the many artists in Art Quilt Network/NY—especially Paula Nadelstern, Margaret Cusack, Dominie Nash, Elizabeth Barton, Linda Levin, Deb Anderson, Liz Axford, Tafi Brown, and Robin Schwalb—for your support and encouragement in the ten-plus years I have come to know you.

Thanks to Karey Bresenhan, for providing the foreword to this book. I would also like to thank Pokey Bolton, Amy Robertson, Janet Yardley, Kristina Almquist, Leslie Rogalski, Shelley Roth, Kenny Wapner, Erika Degens, Sebastian Degens, Monika Ostroff, Nancy Halpern, Robert Shaw, Carol Busby, Nancy Poorvu, Carol Hildebrand, and Kathleen Mahoney for all your kindness and support. If I have neglected to add your name, I thank you nonetheless!

Table of Contents

Foreword

Today, creating quilts that also serve as small journals of life is a rapidly growing movement, one pioneered in 1999 when Jeanne Williamson started making a quilt a week. Her self-assigned projects were uncharted territory in quilting. While other quilt artists have made periodic ventures into creating small quilts on a regular basis, Jeanne's determination and persistence to make a quilt a week for seven years remain unique.

When I created the Journal Quilt Project in 2002, my intention was to encourage quilt artists to break out of the box and try their hands at new quilting methods and techniques, giving themselves new ways to convey the images in their minds. I tied the project to the idea of keeping a working journal that would reflect how the daily occurrences of life—family interactions, weather, location, jobs, and events in the news—affect an artist's work. Instead of completing a quilt a week, as Jeanne was doing, the project called for participants to make one journal quilt per month. The ensuing quilts were then hung at the International Quilt Festival in Houston and Chicago in a striking grid display, with the quilts from each artist displayed horizontally and the quilts from each month displayed vertically. This allowed the viewers to identify any given month and scan down one column to see how the time of year affected the work of many different quilt artists.

As Jeanne has made clear in her book, small art quilts are immensely freeing, since less time and less money are required to make them. In fact, it is the restricted scale of these page-size quilts that encourages quilters to experiment freely with the process and the result before they invest the time, energy, and resources required to make a larger piece. In *The Uncommon Quilter,* Jeanne will not teach you to make heirloom quilts or art quilts for collectors; instead, she will guide you through the process of developing personal-growth pieces that can take you to new levels in your own artistic development.

Virtually any technique can be used successfully in a small mixed-media quilt if the scale of the piece is kept in mind. The artist must exercise self-discipline in limiting his or her choices so the designs remain focused while mastery of the method is achieved. Among the techniques that have been used to good effect are predictable piecing and appliqué along with more unexpected and innovative such as raw edge appliqué, photo-transfer, fusing, discharging, overdyeing, photo expansion, silk fusion, faux felting, layering sheer fabrics, beading, and stamping. When combined with unusual and artistic embellishments, the results are challenging, inspiring, and frequently breathtaking.

Making small quilts on a regular basis, whether weekly or monthly, encourages all artists, experienced or otherwise, to get past the mental and emotional obstacles that occasionally affect every creative person. Focus instead on producing an experimental piece that doesn't have to be right the first time, that doesn't have to win prizes, and that doesn't represent your *pièce de résistance.* Your quilts must reflect your growth only at a particular point in time.

As Jeanne Williamson has demonstrated in her seven years of making weekly quilts, freeing one's imagination from the constraints of expectation is a huge step toward maximizing personal creativity. How delightful it is that for once maximum results can blossom from minimal size!

    —Karey Patterson Bresenhan
    Author, *Creative Quilting: The Journal Quilt Project*
    Director, International Quilt Festival

Introduction

Artists often need to fit their creative time around the rest of their lives, from jobs and family obligations to any of life's other distractions. To create their art, they need to look at—and see—the world around them, and then interpret, translate, and express that information through their medium so others can experience it.

My main focus working as an artist has been with fabric, specifically with making "art quilts," a descendant of folk art quilts that use the entire range of visual arts—including painting, printmaking, photography, and graphic design—to create an aesthetic piece.

I have had the good fortune to exhibit in many galleries and museums around the world. Throughout my career, I have struggled with finding the time to be truly creative, to set aside my preoccupations, and to ignore distractions to experiment with ideas and techniques. For many years, I felt I didn't have the time to sketch, experiment, or just play, and that any time spent creating art had to be used for working on one piece, rather than taking the time to try new things or to make mistakes.

Then, as 1998 was coming to an end, I thought about the opportunity given to me by the new year, and how once again I would struggle to find the time and inspiration to get a small collection of art quilts completed in 1999. About the same time, I visited the studio of a friend from art school who is a painter and sculptor. When I arrived at her studio, not only did she have a really good group of paintings, but she also had piles of small postcard-size drawings and sketches done in ink or watercolor. She had found the time to work, and, even though she didn't think she had produced anything at all, I saw a wonderful progression of creative ideas and images.

After my visit, I spent a lot of time reflecting on how I could give myself more time and permission to "play." After running through several different scenarios, I remembered meeting an artist at my photographer's studio a few years earlier who had decorated a paper sandwich bag every day for a year. I liked the concept but knew that I did not have the time to commit to making something every single day. I decided that I could, however, commit to making something once a week, and that is how my idea to create one small quilt every week was born.

I planned to make the quilts 8" (20cm) wide by 10" (25cm) tall, and to make them anytime during the week. My rules were simple: I could not throw out the original piece and start over with a new one if I didn't like how it was turning out. I would not obsess over the aesthetic of the piece—the goal was to create. There were no limits on what techniques I could use. Each quilt would be dated, numbered, and annotated on the back with details on what was happening in my life or what the quilt was about.

I continued making a quilt a week for seven years, producing a total of 365 pieces. Some took only twenty minutes to create, while others took a few days. As an additional challenge, I decided that with each new year I would change the size of the quilt, providing new design challenges, inspiration, and ideas.

After I finished each quilt, I usually looked forward to starting the next one, and as the pile of quilts grew, I developed a real sense of accomplishment. My creativity also increased, in turn enriching my other more "serious" artwork. I could feel myself growing as an artist. It felt as if a little pipeline were turned on in my head and ideas came steadily bubbling out.

Looking back on the quilts I have made over this seven-year span, I think that many are beautiful and creative. There are also those that I consider badly designed and awkward. But whether certain quilts were good or bad is not the point; the point is that I made the time to try new things, that I took risks, and that I learned a lot. It was one of the best things I ever did for myself, both artistically and personally.

I hope that you will enjoy the creative process, that you will try to make many of the different quilting projects, and that this book will help you discover more about yourself and your art. I encourage you to set aside time for creating, whether it's daily, weekly, or monthly, as it's the only way to stretch your wings, expand your horizons, and grow as an artist.

-Jeanne Williamsom

Getting Started

Whether you're an experienced quilter, a beginning sewer, or a creative artist looking for a new medium, it's always important to experiment with new ideas, techniques, and materials. The more artwork you create, the more you grow and the stronger your work will become.

This book will show you how to make miniature quilts by marrying traditional quilting techniques with unusual materials. Yet it's also designed to help you expand your horizons, find new inspiration, or take risks with your art, whether quilting, sewing, or journaling. Inside these pages you'll find fifty-two projects divided into four categories based on the primary materials and techniques involved: plastic, paper, surface design, and fiber. Each project includes simple step-by-step instructions to produce the quilts pictured in this book. Or you can use them as a jumping-off point for your own projects.

This book is not about making a perfectly crafted traditional quilt. Rather, it is about the process of quilt- and art-making, with the added benefit of changing your perspective as an artist. You will be using recycled materials and unconventional techniques and following few rules when making these miniature quilts. Unlike experienced traditional quilters, who turn under the edges of their appliquéd fabric, sew perfectly spaced stitches, and bind the edges of their quilts, you can leave threads hanging, vary the length of your stitches, or even leave the edges of your work unfinished—the choices are yours to make.

Although my quilts are small (most measure about 8" x 10" [20 x 25cm] or smaller) they are all whole-cloth quilts. When most people hear the word "quilts," they think of patchwork quilts, which are made by sewing many pieces of fabric together. A whole-cloth quilt, however, uses one piece of fabric as the quilt top. This book describes traditional appliqué techniques (sewing pieces of fabric to the quilt top), then pushes the envelope by suggesting that the quilter select unusual objects, such as paper, bark, or pieces of shopping bags, to expand that tradition.

You'll also learn about many other surface design techniques, including crayon rubbings, hand stamping with pencil erasers, hand painting, and purposely painting the back of the quilt so the paint seeps through to the front. Once you have a basic idea of the quilting process, you can consider the icing on the cake, the decorations. Where will your imagination lead you?

The Basics of Creating Small Quilts

If you are thinking about making small quilts on a regular basis, give some thought to what size quilt you will feel comfortable developing. Size is especially important if you are a traditional quilt maker who is used to working on large pieces, as working on a smaller scale may take some adjustment or experimentation. On the other hand, a new scale can be liberating. You may want to experiment with different sizes before you commit to working on one scale. During my seven years of experience in miniature quilt making, 4" x 6" (10 x 15cm) was the smallest size I tried. If you are trying to work small for the first time, I suggest creating a quilt that measures 8" x 10" (20 x 25cm) or a little larger in order to get a feel for the space, materials, and techniques.

As I made the quilts in this book, the time involved varied. Experienced quilters should be able to make most of the quilts in about an hour, though length will vary depending on skill level, materials, and creative inspiration.

This page: "Shredded Evidence," 2002, 6" x 4"

Setting Up Your Workspace

There are a few basic supplies that you will need to have on hand for making any of the projects in this book. Individual projects may call for more specific materials, but, as a general rule, the basic supply list includes the following:

- Cotton fabric (solid white or off-white)
- Cotton quilt batting
- Thread
- Scissors
- Sewing machine (if desired)
- Iron and ironing board, or a towel and a flat surface (Do not leave the iron on and unattended.)
- Laundry pen or permanent marker
- Pencil

You need not buy all new materials to get started—many can be found around your home, at yard sales, in discount stores, or on the Internet (*see* Resources, pages 154–156). For instance, instead of buying cotton fabric, consider cutting up an old solid-colored sheet. Use an old cotton blanket for batting instead of buying cotton quilt batting. If you just want to dabble in miniature quilts, consider borrowing a sewing machine from a friend or neighbor before buying your own. If you prefer to work with your hands, you can hand-stitch your quilts. I prefer a sewing machine for quicker results, but hand-sewn quilts have a very personal look and feel, and in this small format the amount of time and labor involved with hand sewing is not prohibitive; most of the projects in this book can be hand-sewn with no trouble.

Most quilts consist of a sandwich of three layers: fabric on top, quilt batting in the middle, and fabric on the bottom—all of which are sewn together. I recommend cotton quilt batting, not polyester batting, as the thin cotton quilt batting will not slip or shift when sandwiched between two pieces of fabric. For the small quilts in this book, you won't need to baste or pin the "fabric sandwich" together before sewing, which saves time and labor.

This page: "Red and Blue States," 2004, 6" x 7"
Facing page: "Ocean Waves," 1999, 8" x 10"

If you have sewing experience, you may already know that the size of a quilt shrinks somewhat as you sew. Depending on whether you quilt a lot or a little, the amount of shrinkage varies. For best results, start a quilt slightly larger than the desired end product and then trim it to size after sewing. Starting with a larger size also allows flexibility in determining where to center the design (see the "How to Use a Design Template" section for more information, pages 18–19.)

I recommend adding 2" (5cm) to all four sides of the quilt size you are planning to make. If you are planning a finished quilt measuring 8" x 10" (20 x 25cm), for example, cut your fabric and batting pieces to measure 12" x 14" (30 x 30cm). If you are planning to make quilts all the same size, cut identical pieces of fabric and batting. If you cut your pieces ahead of time and store your quilt supplies in a convenient location, then you will always be ready to jump into the creative process at any moment.

Why the Materials Matter

While plenty of materials are specifically designed for quilt-making, endless numbers of natural and synthetic materials are available (many of them free), that you may have never considered using in a quilt. Inspiring and interesting materials can be found in the kitchen, among children's games and toys, and around the yard. You might even cut the tags and labels off new clothing or recycle wrapping paper and ribbon in your projects.

As you go about your daily life, keep your eyes open to the materials around you. You won't need to follow any rules when collecting materials. Anything that gives you an idea for a project is worth keeping. I recommend only two guidelines:

1. Collect mainly materials that you can sew by hand or with a machine.
2. Use materials that won't rot, break, or spoil.

You should not sew food items to a quilt, as they will attract bugs, grow mold, or rot. Natural leaves and flowers are wonderful to use, but most will dry up and crumble. Keep in mind, also, how materials may change over time. On a trip to London, I purchased a piece of clear rubber "fabric," which I used for a few quilts, assuming the material would not degrade. Rubber, however, breaks down, and becomes unpleasant to look at.

If you find small objects that cannot be sewn, such as a shell, a small stick, a flat seed, or a coin, you may be able to find a creative way to attach them to your quilt. Most of your material should be sewable.

As you collect materials, store them in a small box or bag. Keep this container near your quilt supplies. That way, when you find the time to work, you can rummage through your box of objects for inspiration. It's a well-known fact that looking for new ideas or trying new techniques is a great way to fight boredom in your artwork. Notice the seasons changing, acknowledge significant events, or just capture moments of everyday life. As my collection of small quilts expanded, I found it helpful to document each one with the date I created it, or any thoughts or materials that influenced me at the time. If you have a fabric pen or a permanent marker, write a few notes and the date on the back of the quilt—you'll be happy you did.

As you quilt, keep in mind that making mistakes is a valuable learning experience. Sometimes a mistake leads to a new discovery, while other times the process results in creative solutions. Don't throw out your mistakes, as they can be useful for future reference.

Consider structuring your time to create your artwork. Many writers set hours for putting pen to paper; the same can be true for visual artists. If you are looking for new ideas, stop into a craft or fabric store, visit a gallery or a museum, or spend a few quiet hours in your local bookstore or library thumbing through magazines or books. Many artists keep a sketchbook or idea journal in which they collect fabric swatches, drawings, sketches, or photos.

How to Use a Design Template

A template is a guide, or pattern, that helps you play with the size and design of your quilt, and it will save time and labor.

The first year I made weekly quilts, I did not use a template. Instead, I used a ruler to measure out my finished quilt. Not only was that time consuming, but I often ended up with quilts that were not exactly the size I was hoping for. The solution to these problems was to use a template.

I make my templates from thin cardboard, such as the back of a pad of paper or the cardboard packaged with a set of sheets or a men's dress shirt. To make a template, you'll need the following supplies:

- Thin cardboard, larger than the size of the finished quilt (Do not use corrugated cardboard.)
- Pencil
- Ruler
- X-acto knife

Different Sizes of Templates

If you are planning to create small quilts of many sizes, consider making a template for each size.

You can also use a template as a design tool. To change the visual effect of your artwork, for instance, simply change the angle or placement of the design. If you are working with stripes, consider rotating the template so the same stripes are at a different angle. Try playing with the visual presentation of your quilt before cutting it to size and finishing the edges.

Directions for Using a Template

CUTTING A TEMPLATE

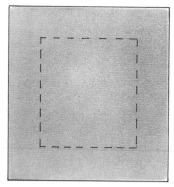

1. Using a ruler and a pencil, draw the quilt size on the cardboard.

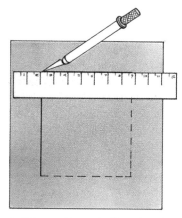

2. Using an X-acto knife and a ruler as your guide, carefully cut along the drawn lines.

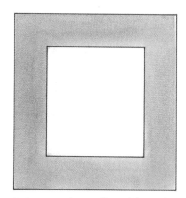

3. Remove the cardboard from the inner area and discard. You now have your template, which should look similar to a picture frame.

Considering Different Angles

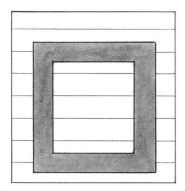

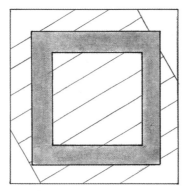

1. After the quilt is sewn, place a template on the quilt top.

2. Holding the template straight, turn the quilt clockwise or counterclockwise to find the desired angle.

Considering Different Placements of Objects

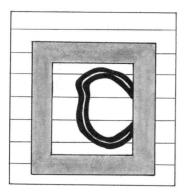

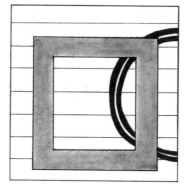

1. Place the template on the quilt top. Move it up, down, or sideways to find the desired placement for the objects in the design.

2. You may want the objects to be centered or off center. By moving the template to different locations on the quilt, you can decide which area you prefer to highlight.

Finishing the Quilts

When you have finished the design and sewing of your quilt, place the correct size template on the quilt top and find the desired angle and placement of your design. Using a pencil, trace the inside edges of the template onto the quilt front to measure the quilt to size. Remove the template and sew a straight stitch ⅛" (.3cm) inside the quilt from the pencil line. Cut the quilt to size on the pencil line using scissors. Sew a zigzag stitch on raw edges to finish.

Plastic

Facing Page:
"Construction Fence,"
2002, 6" x 4"

When you think of quilting, you probably don't think of plastic—especially not to sew with! But plastics come in many forms and can be found in many places, and many of them—particularly if they are thin and flexible enough to sew by machine or by hand—are perfect for use in quilts.

I like sewing with plastic bags because they are similar to fabric but require no finishing or special techniques. The edges will not unravel, the plastic does not need pre-shrinking—as fabric does—and the color will not fade. And since most plastics are usually free, you won't need to worry about quantity or price as you might with fabric purchases. You should, however, make sure the bags you are using are clean; if they aren't, you can wash them with soap and water and hang them to dry.

While the shopping bags I bring home from the grocery store aren't typically special, I have noticed that many retail or clothing stores have beautiful plastic shopping bags. These bags are similar in shape and size to everyday shopping bags and are often made of good, flexible material. One store had a black-and-white-striped bag, while another had semi-opaque multicolored circles, which I cut and used as layers of color (see samples, pages 26 and 28).

If you eat Japanese food, especially sushi, you may have noticed plastic sushi grass on your serving plate or take-out box. Try recycling the grass instead of throwing it away. *Note: Because the grass has been used next to raw fish, it is important to wash it thoroughly with soap and hot water before setting it aside for future use.* Because sushi grass is made of plastic so thin that it resembles paper, it's easy to cut and sew but won't tear like paper.

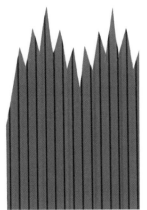

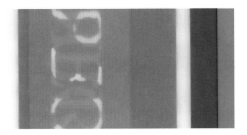

Many retail stores now use beautiful plastic bags for customer purchases.

Sushi grass is a versatile material that can be cut, layered, or embellished to create a wide assortment of effects.

An example of a cut up orange construction fence, which are typically found near bulding construction sites.

If you don't eat sushi but live or work near a Japanese restaurant, ask the sushi chef if he or she will sell you a handful of plastic grass. You can also check gourmet or specialty food supply chains if you want to buy your own.

Absolutely no preparation is needed before you work with plastic grass. Simply take as many clean sheets as you need, plan your design, and organize them on your quilt. I don't recommend pinning the grass to the quilt, however, because once a pin or needle goes into the plastic it will leave a permanent hole.

Have fun with the grass! It's a playful material that works well with fabric, paper, and other embellishments. Consider turning it upside down, cutting it up, layering it (see sample, page 45), or mixing it with other materials to create unique and interesting effects.

If you notice road or building construction near you, see if the site is cordoned off by an orange construction fence. These fences—also called plastic construction fences, snow fences, wind break fences, barrier fences, warning fences, and safety fences—are typically made of plastic and work surprisingly well in quilting.

At first glance, the sizes and shapes of construction fences seem uniform. Yet some have rectangular holes that are vertical or horizontal, or that take the shape of squares, diamonds, or thin ovals. Sometimes the plastic is thick and hard to cut (and will need to be hand sewn), but often it is thin, and therefore easy to machine sew.

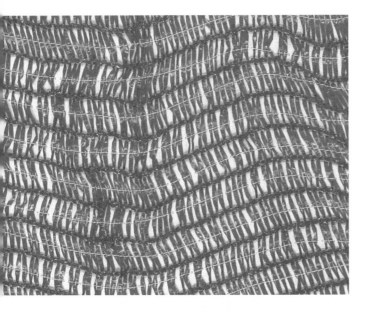

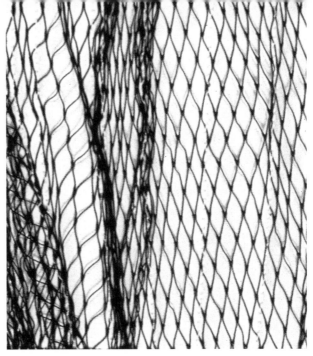

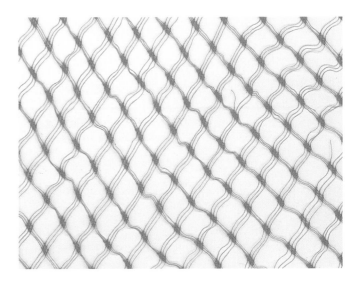

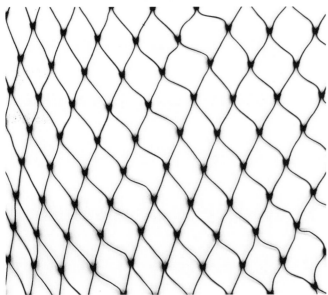

These examples of plastic netting show its diverse appearance: some are very flat and thin, while others may have a thicker dot where the different strands intersect.

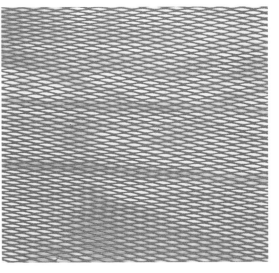

I love the aesthetic simplicity of grids, so I instantly adored construction fences when I first noticed them. After realizing that the grids take many sizes, shapes, and forms, and that the orange plastic sagged in the heat of the sun and cracked in cold temperatures, I was hooked. I currently have a collection of at least fifteen shapes and sizes.

If you want to use pieces of a construction fence in your work, there are a few ways to acquire it. You can go to a building supply store and buy the material, but it is generally sold in quantities of fifty yards or more! Since you will probably use only a few feet of fencing, consider asking for donations. If I see a fence of interest, I take a deep breath, walk up to the construction site, and ask for a piece. (The worst they can say is no!) I keep a strong pair of garden shears in my car for exactly these occasions. With shears in hand, I have talked to sweaty workers on huge construction sites and contractors working on smaller jobs; I have even knocked on the doors of mansions being renovated to ask the owner whether I can have a small section of fencing. I always tell them that I'm an artist and that I will be using it in my artwork, and they are almost always happy to give me a piece. Because these fences are usually destined for the dumpster, many people are more than happy to have them recycled in creative ways.

Be sure to wash your fence and allow it to dry before applying it to your quilt, as chances are it's muddy, dusty, or otherwise dirty. Depending on the size of your piece of fence, you can wash it in the kitchen sink or bathtub; if it's too large to wash indoors, use a hose in your yard. Experiment with construction fences by layering pieces, combining it with other materials, or simply cutting it into scraps as you might paper or magazine images.

Plastic netting, such as the material used in produce bags, is also great quilting material. The bags can include, but are not limited to, those that hold onions, potatoes, limes, lemons, shallots, and oranges. Netting can also be found on the top of a clementine box, where it lets the fruit breathe, or in the garden, where it is sometimes used to cover fruit trees or to help a climbing plant reach greater heights.

Netting comes in a variety of colors, textures, and sizes. I have used many shades of red and yellow, but have also found purple, orange, pink, and white netting. Garden netting tends to come in black or green, with a much larger scale to the pattern.

The size of plastic netting also varies, from 8" x 12" (20 x 30cm) netting bags for onions and small potatoes to 12" x 18" (30 x 45cm) sections used for bags that hold oranges. Garden netting, sometimes found on rolls, can be as wide as 3' (1m) or more.

Depending on your project and your budget, you may want to think twice about investing in several yards of garden netting. The cost of a bag of potatoes, on the other hand, is a better place to start for beginners. As you encounter plastic netting in your everyday use, set it aside.

Sewing plastic netting requires no special care (except for a little patience). Sometimes it gets tangled on itself or on other objects because of its jagged edges. Unlike fabric, you don't need to pre-wash it, and it won't unravel or fray, although you may want to rinse it and allow it to dry before use. Layers of netting can be used for subtle color enhancements and as a design element. You can al Examples of cut up orange construction fences, which are typically found near bulding construction sites. so layer two or more pieces of the same color, or different colors, to create shading and even new hues.

When using netting, relax any need you have for cutting a perfectly shaped piece, as most netting stretches and shrinks with movement. The plastic has a mind of its own, and it will make your life a lot easier if you let the material guide you as you work instead of trying to control it the way you can fabric or paper.

When working with clementine netting, use it as you would a piece of fabric; it feels and moves like cloth, but the edges won't fray. Just cut, stitch, and you're done.

If you're looking for other forms of plastic for your quilts, take a look around your home. The possibilities for inspiration may be as close as the next room!

Plastic netting, found most commonly as the "cloth" in produce bags, is a fun and versatile material with which to sew.

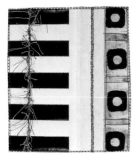

March 2004, 6" x 7" (15 x 17cm)

The interplay of opaque stripes (from a plastic shopping bag), printed fabric, and whimsical yarn softens the overall feel of this quilt.

Striped Bag Collage

MATERIALS

White cotton fabric
(two 10" x 11" [25 x 27.5cm] pieces)

Quilt batting
(one 10" x 11" [25 x 27.5cm] piece)

One $3^{1}/_{2}$" x $7^{1}/_{2}$" (8.7 x 18.7cm) piece of plastic shopping bag with stripes, positioned with stripes horizontally on short end (or substitute a striped fabric)

One $1^{1}/_{2}$" x $7^{1}/_{2}$" (3.8 x 18.7cm) strip of fabric with printed 1" squares (or substitute another geometric print with a plain background)

Two $7^{1}/_{2}$" (18.7cm)-long pieces funky black and white yarn

White thread

Black thread

6" x 7" (15 x 17.5cm) template

INSTRUCTIONS

1. Prepare your quilt by making a sandwich of the top white cotton fabric, the quilt batting, and the bottom white fabric.

2. Place the striped plastic over the top piece of white cotton fabric to the left of the center of the quilt. (A)

3. Using white thread, stitch the striped plastic in place, then stitch around the outline.

4. Place the fabric with squares onto the top piece of white cotton fabric, about $1^{3}/_{4}$" (4.3cm) to the right of the sewn striped plastic. Using black thread, stitch an outline around the piece of fabric with squares. (B)

5. To obtain first $7^{1}/_{2}$" (18.7cm) piece of yarn vertically to the striped section,

sew white or black thread over the yarn using a zigzag stitch. Place the second $7^{1}/_{2}$" (18.7cm) piece of yarn vertically over the white section of quilt top, measuring 1" (2.5cm) from the right edge of the stripes. Attach the yarn to the quilt using a straight stitch in white or black thread. (C)

6. Place the 6 x 7" (15 x 17.5cm) template on quilt top to find the desired angle and placement of design.

7. To cut the quilt to size and finish the edges, refer to the "Finishing the Quilts" instructions in the "Getting Started" section on page 19. Use black thread when sewing straight and zigzag stitches.

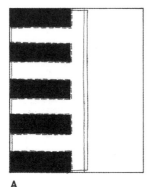

A

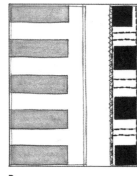

B

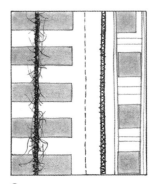

C

February 2005, 6" x 8" (15 x 20 cm)

Drawing inspiration from a neighbor's sheer shopping bag, I went to work on a quilt that would mimic the use of sheer fabric. I overlapped the semi-opaque colors and shapes from the bag with fabric for an even more complex, layered design.

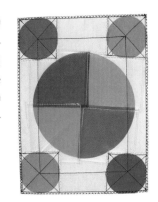

Circle Collage

MATERIALS

White cotton fabric
(two 10" x 12" [25 x 30cm] pieces)

Quilt batting
(one 10" x 12" [25 x 30cm] piece)

Four square patches, each with a different colored circle, cut from plastic shopping bag (or substitute cut fabric circles from leftover sheer fabric)

Four smaller square patches of opaque fabric circles

White thread

Black thread

6" x 8" (15 x 20cm) template

INSTRUCTIONS

1. Prepare your quilt by making a sandwich of the top white cotton fabric, the quilt batting, and the bottom white fabric.

2. Quarter the four square patches of different colored circles, choosing one pie-shaped quarter from each. Place the four pie-shaped sections of colored circles in the center of the top piece of white cotton fabric. Slightly overlap each of the flat edges, re-creating a full circle. (A)

3. Following the exposed edges of the pie sections, stitch the four overlapping pie-shaped sections in place, using white thread.

4. Place the 6" x 8" (15 x 20cm) template on the quilt top, centering the circle you just stitched. Place one square patch with a circle on the quilt at each corner of the template. Pin the patches and remove the template.

5. Sew a zigzag stitch over the edges of the patches using white thread. (B)

6. Using black thread, sew a straight stitch over the edges of the corner patches, sewing over the white zigzag stitching. Then, stitch a black *x* through each of the corner square patches. Stitch a box around the large center circle, with each of the corners of the box touching the center of the *x*'s in each corner square. (C)

7. Place the 6" x 8" (15 x 20cm) template on the quilt top to find the desired angle and placement of design.

8. To cut the quilt to size and finish the edges, refer to the "Finishing the Quilts" instructions in the "Getting Started" section on page 19. Use black thread when sewing straight and zigzag stitches.

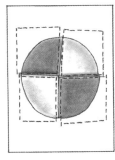

A

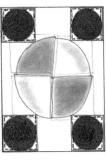

B

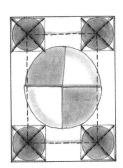

C

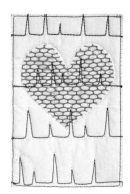

January 2001, 4" x 6" (10 x 15cm)

Sometimes creative ideas are hiding in plain sight. In my kitchen, I noticed a piece of red plastic netting that covered a box of clementine oranges. It actually feels and moves like a piece of fabric. The discovery practically gave me heart palpitations—the subject of this quilt.

Heartbeat

MATERIALS

White cotton fabric
(two 8" x 10" [20 x 25cm] pieces)

Quilt batting (one 8" x 10"
[20 x 25cm] piece)

Red netting from
clementine box top

White thread

Black quilting thread

4" x 6" (10 x 15cm) template

INSTRUCTIONS

1. Fold the red netting from the clementine box in half and cut a heart shape to 1½" (3.7cm) wide by 3" (7.5cm) tall. **(A)**

2. Prepare your quilt by making a sandwich of the top white cotton fabric, quilt batting, and the bottom white fabric.

3. Open the cut heart shape, place it on the center of top piece of white cotton fabric, and sew the heart in place using a straight stitch and white thread around its outline. **(B)**

4. With black quilting thread, sew the heartbeats from left to right, making long, straight lines with jagged upward peaks, interrupting the line as you wish.

Repeat each row of "heartbeats" a total of four lines. Height of peaks can reach from ⅜" (1 cm) to 1" (2.5cm) tall, spaced randomly from ⅜" (1 cm) to ¾" (1.9 cm). **(C)**

5. Place the 4" x 6" (10 x 15cm) template on quilt top to horizontally center placement of the heart. The bottom of the heart should be 2" (5cm) from the quilt bottom.

6. To cut the quilt to size and finish the edges, refer to the "Finishing the Quilts" instructions in the "Getting Started" section on page 19. Use black thread for straight stitches and white thread for zigzag stitches.

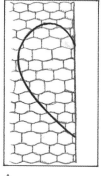

A

B

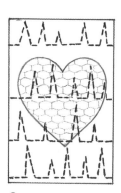

C

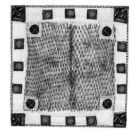

January 2003, 6" x 6" (15 x 15cm)

Amish quilts have a particularly charming combination of symmetry and simplicity. Their geometric patterns and rich colors evoke a calm that I wanted to replicate. Using an onion bag and fabric scraps, I created my own oasis.

Amish Influence

MATERIALS

White cotton fabric
(two 10" x 10" [25 x 25cm] pieces)

Quilt batting
(one 10" x 10" [25 x 25cm] piece)

Onion netting bag

Four ¾" x ¾" (1.8 x 1.8cm) squares of fabric

Twelve ½" x ½" (1.2 x 1.2cm) squares of fabric

Four ¾" x ¾" (1.8 x 1.8cm) fabric square patches, with smaller circles printed on patch (purple circles on white shown)

White thread

6" x 6" (15 x 15cm) template

INSTRUCTIONS

1. Cut two pieces of netting, approximately 4" (10cm) square.

2. Prepare your quilt by making a sandwich of the top white cotton fabric, quilt batting, and the bottom white fabric. Place one square piece of netting on top of the other and pin the two pieces in place in the center of the quilt sandwich.

3. Stitch in place using white thread and a straight stitch. If the netting wants to fold back on itself a bit, don't worry—this will give you more "color." **(A)**

4. Sew one each of four ¾" x ¾" (1.8 x 1.8cm) fabric squares in the corners of the quilt using a zigzag stitch. **(B)**

5. Evenly space three of the twelve ½" x ½" (1.2 x 1.2cm) squares of fabric in a row on all perimiters of the quilt between the corner pieces you applied in the previous step. Pin the twelve pieces and stitch in place using white thread. **(C)**

6. Pin the four ¾" x ¾" (1.8 x 1.8cm) square patches with smaller circles printed on the patch to the inside corners of the large netting square. Sew in place using a zigzag stitch and white thread.

7. To add more decoration and to secure the netting section to the quilt, stitch white thread diagonally over the entire design from corner to corner, creating an "X." Then stitch both vertically and horizontally, creating a "+." Add more decorative white stitched lines if desired. **(D)**

8. Place the 6" x 6" (15 x 15cm) template on quilt top to find the desired angle and placement of design.

9. To cut the quilt to size and finish the edges, refer to the "Finishing the Quilts" instructions in the "Getting Started" section on page 19. Use black thread when sewing straight and zigzag stitches.

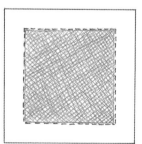

A

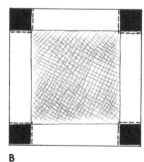

B

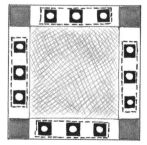

C

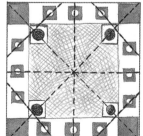

D

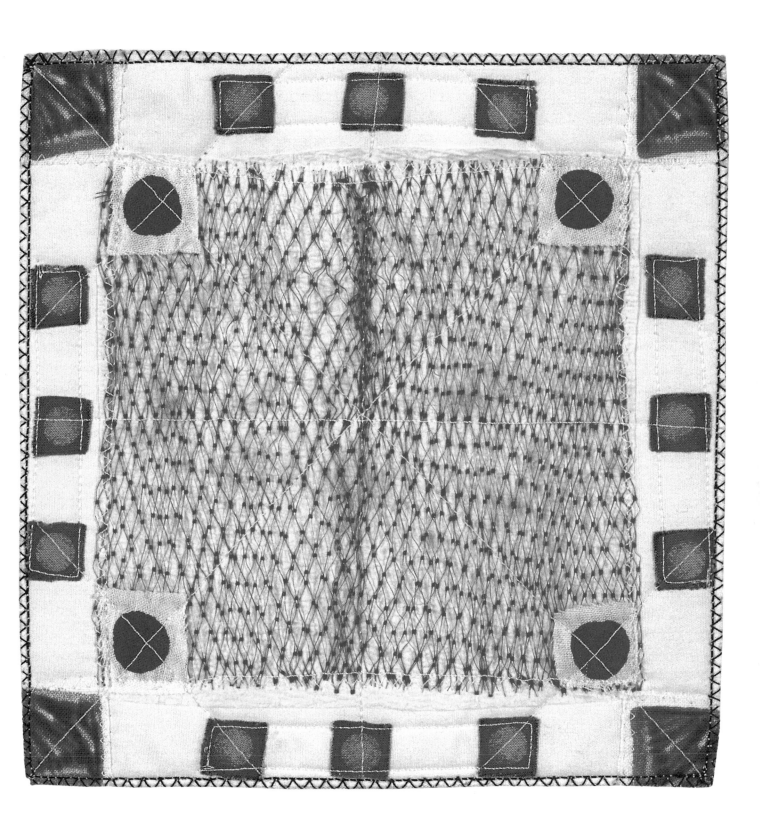

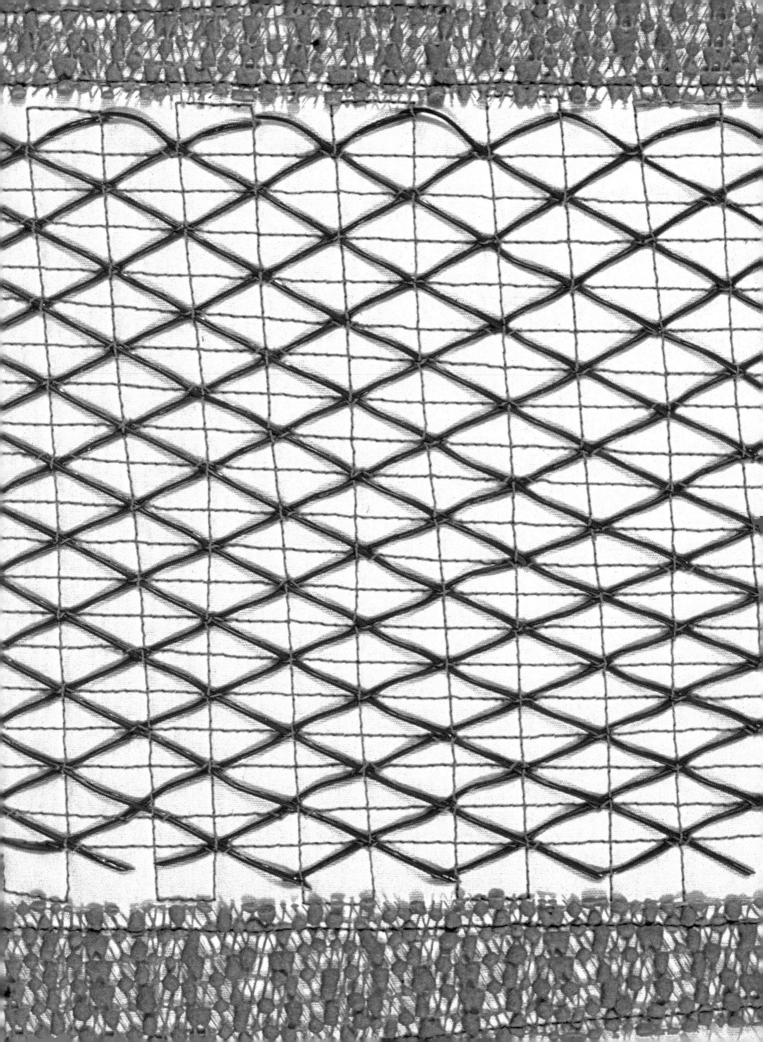

I love unusual recycled objects, such as the green plastic used in this quilt. Its texture reminded me of the interplay between synthetic materials and the natural objects that they represent.

Green Design

MATERIALS

White cotton fabric
(two 10" x 11" [25 x 27.5cm] pieces)

Quilt batting (one 10" x 11"
[25 x 27.5cm] piece)

One 4 ¾" x 6½" (11.8 x 16.2cm) piece of colored and textured netting (e.g., fruit netting, onion bags, wine bags, etc.)

Two 1" x 3" (2.5 x 7.5cm) scraps of yellow onion netting bag

Two 6½" x 1¼" (16.2 x 3.1cm) pieces of non-skid rug padding from discarded rug or green plastic netting

White thread

Black thread

Green quilting thread

6" x 7" (15 x 17.5cm) template

INSTRUCTIONS

1. Prepare your quilt by making a sandwich of the top white cotton fabric, the quilt batting, and the bottom white fabric.

2. Sew the 4¾" x 6½" (16.2 x 3.1cm) piece of netting to the middle section of the quilt top.

3. Using a contrasting thread color, stitch horizontally and vertically across the diagonal grid of the netting, creating a "+" pattern. **(A)**

4. Place the two 6½" x 1¼" (16.2 x 3.1cm) pieces of non-skid rug padding strips on the top and bottom edges of the quilt horizontally. **(B)**

5. Place the pieces of yellow netting under the rug padding, slightly off center.

6. Hand-stitch the layered strips of yellow netting and rug padding to the quilt top and bottom edges of the quilt horizontally, using green quilting thread. *Note: The rug underlay can be thick and is often difficult to sew by machine. For ease of sewing, stitch by hand.* **(C)**

7. Place the 6" x 7" (15 x 17.5cm) template on the quilt top to find the desired angle and placement of design.

8. To cut the quilt to size and finish the edges, refer to the "Finishing the Quilts" instructions in the "Getting Started" section on page 19. Use black thread when sewing straight and zigzag stitches.

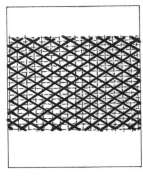

A

B

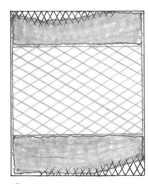

C

February 2005, 6" x 7" (15 x 17.5cm)

I saw Christo and Jeanne-Claude's *Gates* (an installation of 7,500 bright orange gates) in New York City's Central Park in February 2005. Their planned yet ephemeral quality—the *Gates* were displayed only for a few weeks—was made magical by the alternately snowy and sunny weather during their exhibition.

Netting Gates

MATERIALS

White cotton fabric
(two 10" x 11" [25 x 27.5cm] pieces)

Quilt batting
(one 10" x 11" [25 x 27.5cm] piece)

One $1^1/_2$" x $6^1/_2$" (3.7 x 16.2cm) piece of blue ribbon with silver edges (or substitute a plain piece of blue ribbon)

One $2^1/_2$" x $6^1/_2$" (6.2 x 16.2cm) piece of green ribbon with gold edges (or substitute a plain piece of green ribbon)

Orange onion bag netting bag, cut into one $1^1/_4$" x 1" (3.1 x 2.5cm) piece and one 1" x $^3/_4$" (2.5 x 1.8cm) piece

One white onion netting bag

White thread

Black thread

Orange thread

6" x 7" (15 x 17.5cm) template

INSTRUCTIONS

1. Prepare your quilt by making a sandwich of the top white cotton fabric, the quilt batting, and the bottom white fabric.

2. Sew green ribbon near the bottom edge of the quilt top, using white thread and a straight stitch.

3. Sew blue ribbon $3^1/_4$" (1.8cm) above the green ribbon, toward the top edge of the quilt, using white thread and a straight stitch. **(A)**

4. Pin the two pieces of orange onion bag netting on the quilt top between the two ribbons. Add a layer of white netting over the orange netting pieces. Using white thread, sew diagonal lines over the netting. Add white netting on top of the first layer for more complex shading.

I sewed diagonal lines to mimic the pattern of falling snow. **(B)**

5. Stitch lines of orange thread from the green ribbon toward the orange netting. Pivot, sewing horizontally across the top, and pivot again toward the green ribbon. This provides a visual cue to the gate's framework. **(C)**

6. Place the 6" x 7" (15 x 17.5cm) template on quilt top to find the desired angle and placement of design.

7. To cut the quilt to size and finish the edges, refer to the "Finishing the Quilts" instructions in the "Getting Started" section on page 19. Use black thread when sewing straight and zigzag stitches.

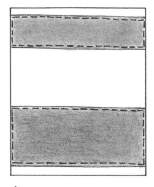

A

B

C

June 2005, 6" x 7" (15 x 17.5cm)

The red sack used in creating this quilt was made using an old lace technique, when the delicate material was made by twisting or knotting threads.

Red Design

MATERIALS

White cotton fabric
(two 10" x 11" [25 x 27.5cm] pieces)

Quilt batting
(one 10" x 11" [25 x 27.5cm] piece)

One piece of red sack
or netting, 6½" x 7"
(16.2 x 17.5cm)

One piece of 1½" (3.7cm)-wide
red ribbon, 6½" (16.2cm) long,
with or without dots

White thread

Black thread

6" x 7" (15 x 17.5cm) template

INSTRUCTIONS

1. Prepare your quilt by making a sandwich of the top white cotton fabric, the quilt batting, and the bottom white fabric.

2. Place a 6½" x 7" (16.2 x 17.5cm) piece of red sack or netting in the center of the top piece of white cotton fabric. Sew a straight stitch between rows found on the netting, using white thread. **(A)**

3. Place the red ribbon horizontally on the quilt top, slightly touching the top edge of the netting.

4. Sew rows of straight stitches horizontally across ribbon, as desired, for decoration. **(B)**

5. Place the 6" x 7" (15 x 17.5cm) template on quilt top to find the desired angle and placement of design.

6. To cut the quilt to size and finish the edges, refer to the "Finishing the Quilts" instructions in the "Getting Started" section on page 19. Use black thread when sewing straight and zigzag stitches.

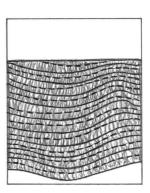

A

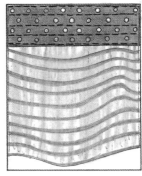

B

July 2005, 6" x 8" (15 x 20cm)

The delicate netting used to bundle oranges and other stone fruits has a surprising charm. I discovered upon close inspection that the thin strips of red plastic were woven rather than fused. The bag's black woven handle was a welcome addition to my design.

Red Bag, Black Handle

MATERIALS

White cotton fabric
(two 10" x 11" [25 x 27.5cm] pieces)

Quilt batting
(one 10" x 11" [25 x 27.5cm] piece)

One piece of 3" x 9" (7.5 x 22.5cm) black onion bag netting

One 6" x 8 " (15 x 20cm) piece of red netting from a bag of oranges (including the black handle)

Black thread

White thread

6" x 8" (15 x 20cm) template

INSTRUCTIONS

1. Prepare your quilt by making a sandwich of the top white cotton fabric, the quilt batting, and the bottom white fabric.

2. With left edge at the center, place black netting on right side of the quilt top. Pin or secure in place, if desired. **(A)**

3. With the black handle vertical on the left edge, place the netting from the bag of oranges on the quilt, covering the black netting.

4. Using white thread, sew straight stitches vertically between every few rows of the netting. Start the stitching from the top of the red net and stitch to the bottom edge. **(B)**

5. Place the 6" x 8" (15 x 20cm) template on quilt top to find the desired angle and placement of design.

6. To cut the quilt to size and finish the edges, refer to the "Finishing the Quilts" instructions in the "Getting Started" section on page 19. Use black thread when sewing straight and zigzag stitches.

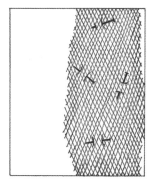

A

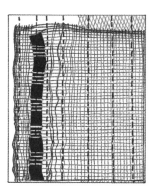

B

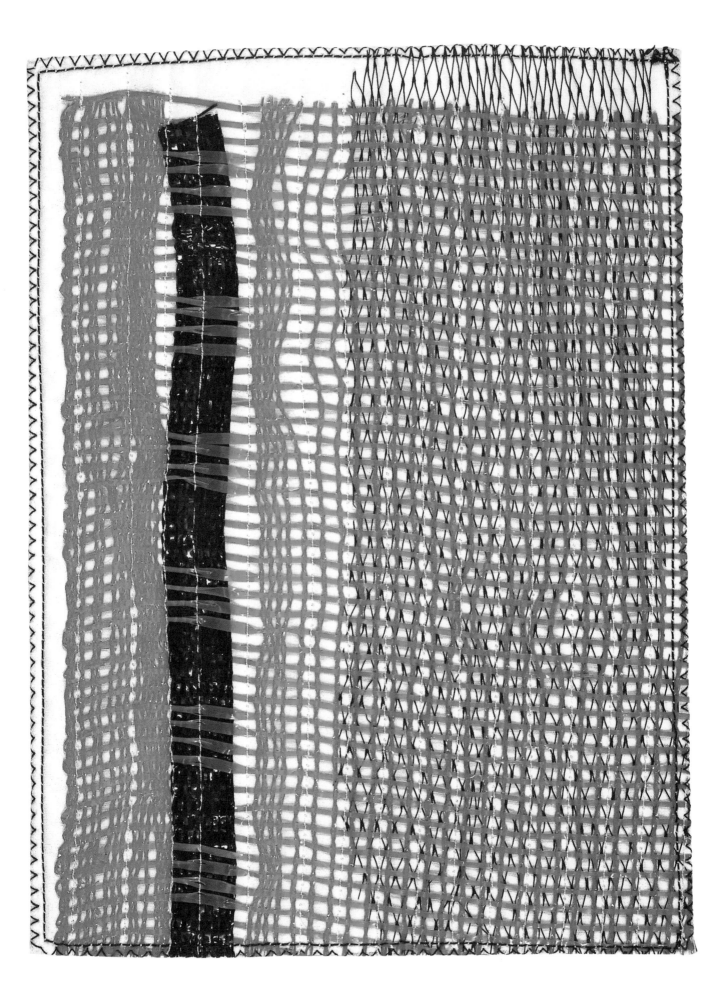

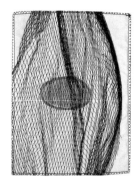

July 2005, 6" x 8" (15 x 20cm)

Onion netting bags are usually stitched together at both ends, but for this quilt, I cut the bag open, giving it a chance to fold back on itself and create an interplay of shading and form.

Free-Form Netting

MATERIALS

White cotton fabric
(two 10" x 11" [25 x 27.5cm] pieces)

Quilt batting
(one 10" x 11" [25 x 27.5cm] piece)

Red fabric oval or circle
(1½" x 2½" [3.7 x 6.2cm] oval shown)

Black onion netting bag (whole bag)

White thread

6" x 8" (15 x 20cm) template

INSTRUCTIONS

1. Prepare your quilt by making a sandwich of the top white cotton fabric, the quilt batting, and the bottom white fabric.

2. Place the red oval or circle in the center of the quilt top and pin in place, if desired. (A)

3. Cut the closed ends off the black onion netting bag, and also cut along the long end of the bag, opening it up.

4. Open the netting bag to about 6" wide at the middle of its length, then place it on the top piece of white cotton fabric, covering the red oval or circle. Do not force the netting to be too flat or wide; instead, let it stay narrow on the ends. Don't be concerned whether parts of the netting are lumpy or sticking up. Pin in place if necessary.

5. Sew a straight stitch from the top of the quilt to the bottom, using white thread. Stitch rows randomly, or along the overlapped sections of netting, to hold it in place and to create more texture. (B)

6. Place the 6" x 8" (15 x 20cm) template on quilt top to find the desired angle and placement of design.

7. To cut the quilt to size and finish the edges, refer to the "Finishing the Quilts" instructions in the "Getting Started" section on page 19. Use black thread when sewing straight and zigzag stitches.

A

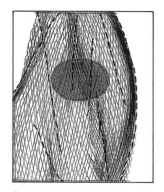

B

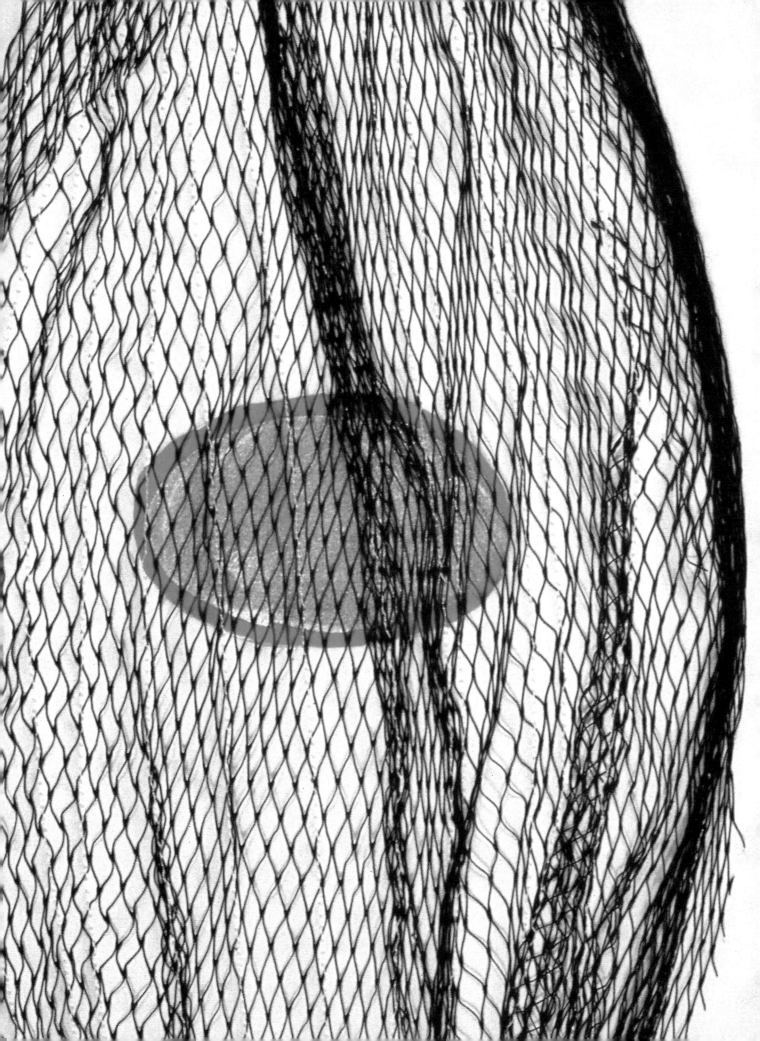

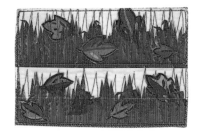

November 2002, 6" x 4" (15 x 10cm)

The irony of pairing impervious plastic with a breathable, printed cotton in a natural theme brought a light mood to this quilt, which I made as the leaves were changing colors in my New England town.

Autumn Leaves

MATERIALS

White cotton fabric
(two 10" x 8" [25 x 20cm] pieces)

Quilt batting
(one 10" x 8" [25 x 20cm] piece)

Four pieces of plastic sushi grass
(or substitute two pieces of
1¾" x 6½" (4.3 x 16.2cm) green
paper, cut with jagged edges on
the horizontal edge to resemble
thick blades of grass)

Eight small fabric leaves,
cut from printed fabric

Black thread

White thread

Green thread

6" x 4" (15 x 10cm) template

INSTRUCTIONS

1. Prepare your quilt by making a sandwich of the top white cotton fabric, the quilt batting, and the bottom white fabric.

2. Position two rows of two sheet–wide sections of plastic sushi grass (or substitute cut green paper) horizontally across the quilt top vertically 2" (5 cm) apart. **(A)**

3. Randomly place four leaves on each of the two rows. Pin or hold leaves and grass in place. **(B)**

4. Using green thread, sew straight stitches up and down across the quilt, over the two rows of sushi grass and fabric leaves to create thread-like blades of grass. **(C)**

5. Place the 6" x 4" (15 x 10cm) template on quilt top to find the desired angle and placement of design.

6. To cut the quilt to size and finish the edges, refer to the "Finishing the Quilts" instructions in the "Getting Started" section on page 19. Use black thread when sewing straight and white thread for zigzag stitches.

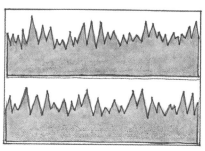

A

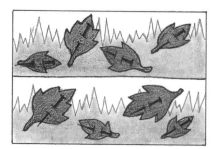

B

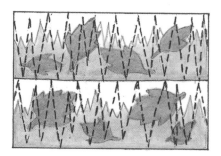

C

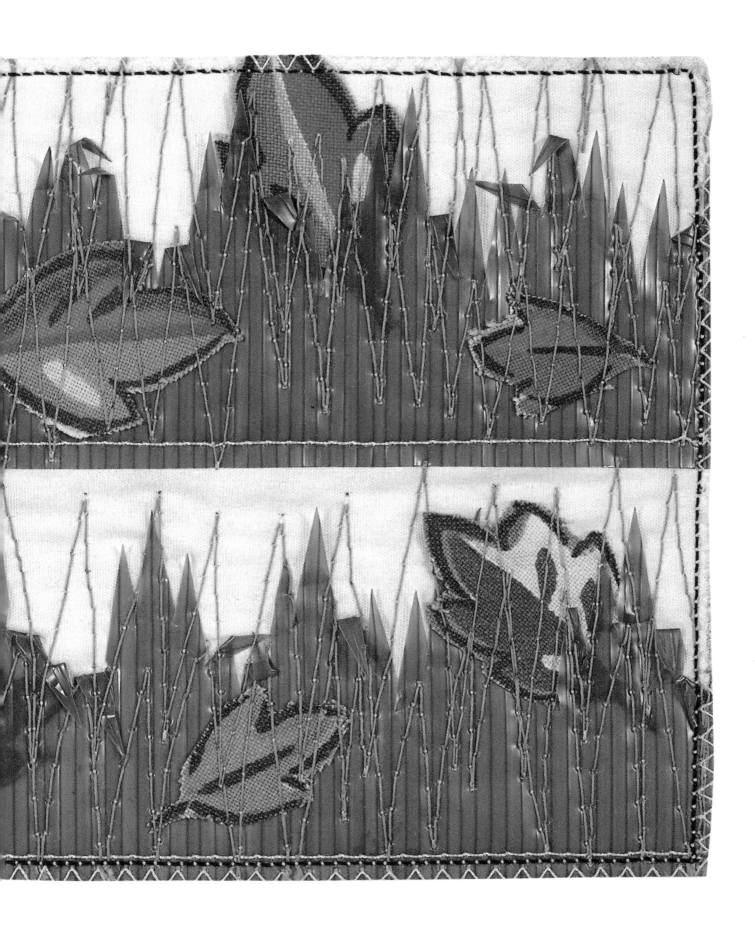

March 2002, 6" x 4" (15 x 10cm)

Orange construction fences, while made from plastic, look like fabric with holes that vary in size and shape. This quilt combines a piece of orange construction fence with a crayon rubbing of the same piece of fence.

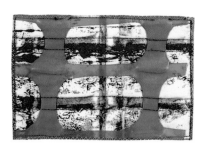

Construction Fence

MATERIALS

White cotton fabric
(two 10" x 8" [25 x 20cm] pieces)

Quilt batting (one 10" x 8" [25 x 20cm] piece)

Wide black crayon

One 7" x 5" (17.5 x 12.5cm) piece orange construction fence

One larger piece of the same construction fence to use for a crayon rubbing

Iron and ironing board (or substitute iron and towel)

Black thread

6" x 4" (15 x 10cm) template

Optional:

Small jar of black fabric paint

Small, inexpensive paintbrush

INSTRUCTIONS

1. Using the fabric that will be the quilt top, create a crayon rubbing of a piece of the construction fence. (A) *Note: See the instructions for creating crayon rubbings on fabric in the "Surface Design" chapter on page 85.*

2. If the crayon rubbing is not dark enough for you, try painting the crayon rubbing area with fabric paint to enhance it. *Note: See the instructions for working with fabric paint in the "Surface Design" chapter on page 86.*

3. Prepare your quilt by making a sandwich of crayon rubbing as the top fabric, the quilt batting, and the bottom white fabric. (B)

4. Place the 7" x 5" (17.5 x 12.5cm) piece of construction fence on the quilt top, positioning it off center from the crayon rubbing. Using a heavy sewing machine needle and black thread, sew straight stitches along the edges of the rubbing design, stitching over the construction fence. (C)

5. Place the 6" x 4" (15 x 10cm) template on the quilt top to find the desired angle and placement of design.

6. To cut the quilt to size and finish the edges, refer to the "Finishing the Quilts" instructions in the "Getting Started" section on page 19. Use black thread when sewing straight and white thread for zigzag stitches.

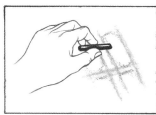

A

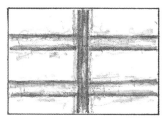

B

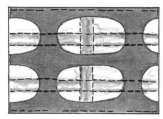

C

August 2001, 4" x 6" (10 x 15cm)

While on vacation in London, I hand-stitched a few small pieces of colored glass, a coin, and a ripped section of a castle brochure onto a piece of fabric. You can do this on any vacation with minimal materials for a very personal memento.

London Vacation

MATERIALS

White cotton fabric
(two 8" x 10" [20 x 25cm] pieces)

Quilt batting
(one 8" x 10" [20 x 25cm] piece)

Small, flat memorabilia
collected from a trip

Travel sewing supplies:

Needles

White thread

Black thread

Travel scissors
*Note: Check federal
regulations before you pack*

4" x 6" (10 x 15cm) template

INSTRUCTIONS

1. Before leaving on a trip, prepare your quilt by making a sandwich of the top white cotton fabric, the quilt batting, and the bottom white fabric.

2. Pack travel sewing supplies in checked baggage.

3. As you travel, collect small, flat items to sew on your quilt: plastic bags or wrappers from your utensils on the airplane, coins, pieces of fabric if you go fabric shopping, a coffee stirrer, small pieces of cardboard, small sections of a travel brochure or tourist information, ticket stubs, postcards, stamps, and so on.

4. If you collect items that are impossible to sew, wrap scraps of a plastic bag around them and sew them randomly to the quilt. (See photograph for examples of sewn plastic bags or wrapping.) Small, thin art items can also be attached by sewing small stitches around the objects. **(A)**

5. To find the desired angle and placement of design, place the 4" x 6" (10 x 15cm) template on quilt top.

6. To cut the quilt to size and finish the edges, refer to the "Finishing the Quilts" instructions in the "Getting Started" section on page 19. Sew a second line of straight stitches ⅛" (.3cm) inside the first line. Use black thread when sewing straight stitches and white thread for zigzag stitches.

A

TOWER

Paper

Paper is a ubiquitous part of our lives; yet many of us fail to see the beauty in either the paper itself or what is printed on the paper unless it's officially labeled as "art." As you come across paper during your day, look at its texture, and examine what is printed on it. Does it have any qualities that may be useful in your quilts? If the color, content, texture, size, or hand-feel appeals to you, save it.

Keep these tips in mind: Thinner papers can be problematic when sewn. If the stitches are too small, they may cause the paper to rip. Stiffer papers, on the other hand, can withstand needle and thread and offer an interesting, often unique, texture.

Remember that regardless of paper weight, once you sew through a piece of paper, the needle hole will be there forever. Stop to think before you sew, and experiment until you are comfortable with the material.

Facing page: "Cupcake Design," 2002, 6" x 4"

Building Your Paper Collection

Have you ever noticed how many slips of paper, receipts, or ticket stubs you accumulate when you travel?

These small reminders are perfect for making a "memory quilt." Be sure to save your plane, train, and event tickets; boarding passes; bus or train schedules; pretty paper bags from purchases; and maps and travel brochures. You may want to cut these items into smaller pieces and enclose them under netting, slip them into sheer pockets, or make color copies onto heavier paper stock and sew them directly onto your quilt.

Postcards of art offer many interesting ideas for collage.

This patchwork grid of giftwrap mixes different patterns but similar colors.

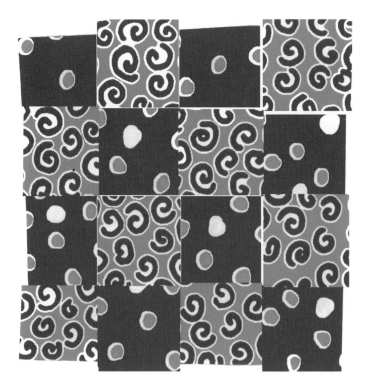

Postcards and magazines are cornerstones of a good paper collection. Postcards, whether from a tourist destination or a gallery exhibit, are worth saving. Similarly, clipped magazine images pieced together to form a larger design—as if you were using pieces of fabric—make for an intriguing visual statement.

Every paper collection should have an assortment of wrapping paper, both recycled and new. To store this material, cut the paper into smaller pieces or cut out the prettiest sections and store them flat. When you use the wrapping paper in a quilt (see sample, page 72) not only will you have a beautiful quilt, but you'll also have a wonderful memory of the gift you have received or given.

Every paper collection should have an assortment of wrapping paper, both recycled and new. To store this material, cut the paper into smaller pieces or cut out the prettiest sections and store them flat. When you use the wrapping paper in a quilt (see sample, page 72) not only will you have a beautiful quilt, but you'll also have a wonderful memory of the gift you have received or given.

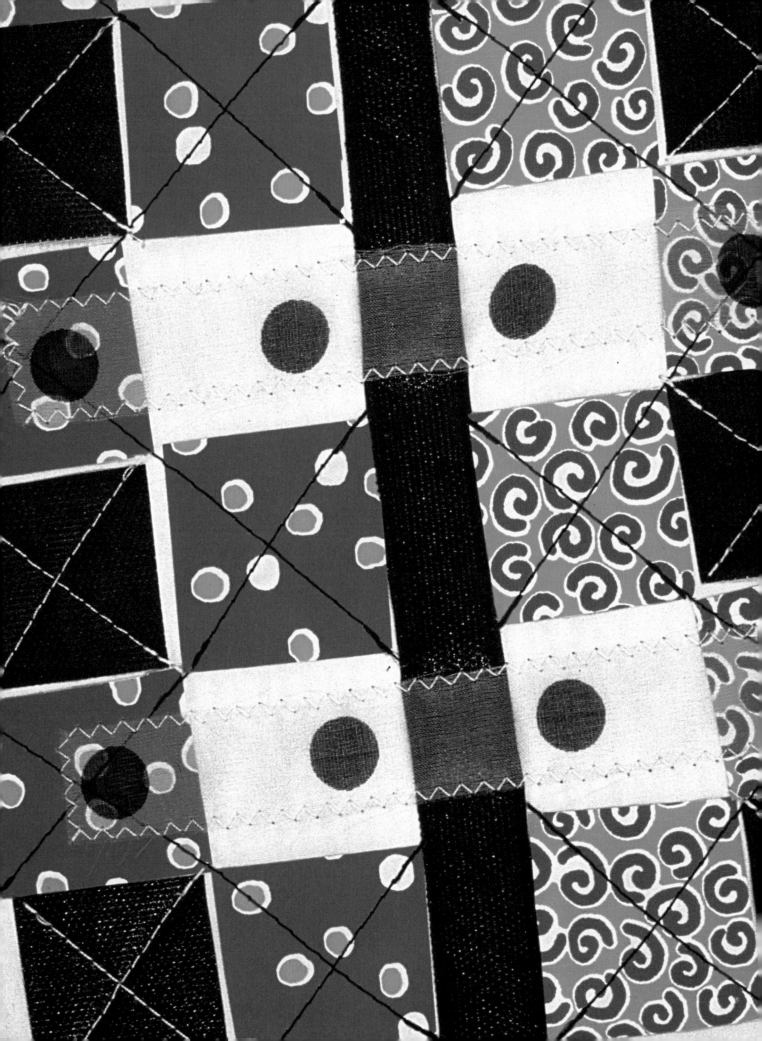

Previous page: "Recycled Patchwork," 2004, 6" x 7"

I also like to use facial tissues in my quilts. Decorative facial tissues are more like fabric than paper. Look for small packets of printed tissues at your drugstore or grocery store. If you see a design you like, try sewing with it, either using them whole as a background or cut up and combined with scraps of fabric to create a beautiful collage.

Have you ever received a newspaper that was torn during printing or delivery? The tears may be dramatic, with ragged edges that look like icicles (see sample, page 66). Why let a machine-made—but natural-looking—shape go to waste? Torn newspaper offers many design possibilities. Consider using two torn edges to make a design on adjacent angles, interweaving sections or layering pieces to create the illusion of depth.

If you've ever used a sticker for mailing or for a children's project, you're no doubt familiar with the templates left behind once the stickers have been removed. You can use the grid, with its missing shapes, in a variety of ways. Small scraps of fabric can be sewn in the holes, or you can draw or paint inside them. If you apply the sticker leftovers to your fabric, be sure to stitch them in place as adhesives usually break down over time.

Cupcake wrappers, such as the ones shown on page 64, can be very pretty additions to a quilt. (Be on the lookout for round wrappers as well as for oval shapes.) If you have clean and interesting wrappers, you can stitch them directly to your fabric. Your kitchen may also contain other paper materials for your quilts, including coffee filters, doilies, parchment paper, wax paper, and paper towels, to name just a few.

Torn newspaper is another versatile material for use in quilts.

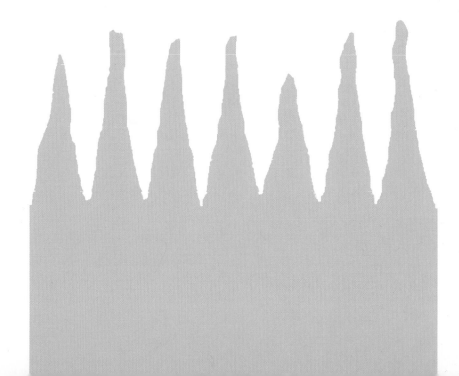

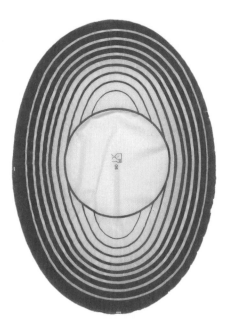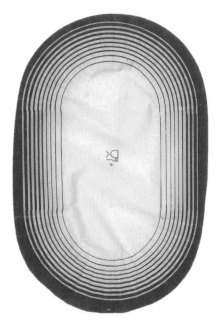

If you have a paper frame or mat that was protecting a photograph, you can use it as a template to measure your quilts, or you can cut and sew it to your fabric. Many mats have a gold stripe or a bas-relief near the edge that offers a nice design element.

Many coffee shops use hot beverage sleeves. While the outside of the sleeves might be constructed of plain cardboard, the inside is usually made of corrugated cardboard. No matter what you find inside, these sleeves can be used for textured crayon rubbings or for sewing onto a quilt. Use them whole or cut them into pieces.

Packaged potatoes often come in a paper bag with a netted window to keep the potatoes fresh and secure. Once empty, the bag offers an assortment of design possibilities. Consider placing fabric or paper behind the net window, and then sew the netting in place.

Black landscaping fabric is designed to keep weeds and unwanted plants from growing in a garden by blocking light and creating a barrier to growth. While not really paper or fabric in a conventional sense, this black "cloth" is easy to cut and sew, and it works well in mixed-media quilts.

Cupcake holders come in many different shapes, sizes, and colors and can be used in quiltmaking.

Paper maps can be used on a quilt to create texture, to document a place that you love, or to add beautiful colors and designs to your quilts. Simply find the section of the map that you want to use, cut it to size, and stitch it in place. Consider sewing a sheer fabric on top of it to change the color, or cut the map into small pieces and create a patchwork design, similar to the technique shown on page 72 with wrapping paper.

Bar codes might be used by businesses for tracking inventory and sales, but for your purposes they can be used as a design element. They can be found on almost any product: Magazines, cereal boxes, and even airline boarding passes. Though small, groups of different bar codes can be used together to make a design—shown on page 75—or one can be used alone.

Printing photographs on photo paper can be costly. Consider printing images on regular paper and then sew them to your quilt. Simply print out the photo you want to use, trim it to the desired size or shape, and stitch it in place.

If you are interested in using other paper in your quilts, start by looking around your home: Books, cardboard coasters, paper plates, children's board games, or playing cards are just the beginning. The possibilities are truly endless!

Facing page: "College Drop-Off," 2004, 6" x 7"

Barcodes can be used alone, but their uniformity makes them especially useful for creating repetitive patterns.

January 2002, 6" x 4" (15 x 10cm)

While on a trip to New York City, I collected fabric and postcards, many of which had a black-and-white theme. I cut them into a duotone grid, mimicking the polarized feel of the city, while paying homage to the overarching grid that governs the ebb and flow of urban life.

Black & White Squares

MATERIALS

White cotton fabric
(two 10" x 8" [25 x 20cm] pieces)

Quilt batting
(one 10" x 8" [25 x 20cm] piece)

Six 2" (5cm) square pieces of black and white postcards, paper, or fabric

Black thread

White thread

6" x 4" (15 x 10cm) template

INSTRUCTIONS

1. Collect postcards, pieces of paper, or scraps of fabric that look good together. Choose similar color schemes or a coordinating design.

2. Prepare your quilt by making a sandwich of the top white cotton fabric, the quilt batting, and the bottom white fabric.

3. Arrange the six 2" (5cm) square pieces on the quilt top in two rows of three squares.

4. Sew around the edges of each square, attaching the six squares to the quilt using black zigzag stitches. **(A)**

5. Place the 6" x 4" (15 x 10cm) template on the quilt top to find the desired angle and placement of design.

6. To cut the quilt to size and finish the edges, refer to the "Finishing the Quilts" instructions in the "Getting Started" sectionon page 19. Use black thread when sewing straight and white thread for the zigzag stitches.

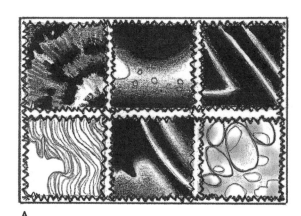

A

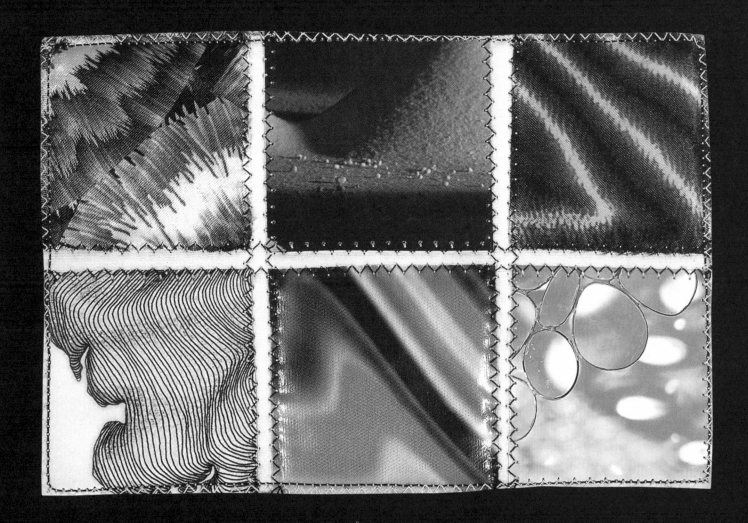

January 2002, 6" x 4" (15 x 10cm)

Modern technology is often liberating, but in the case of Enron, it was simply excess. In an effort to conserve, I made this quilt using cut strips of fabric with text, then added shredded paper on top.

Shredded Evidence

MATERIALS

White cotton fabric
(two 10" x 8" [25 x 20cm] pieces)

Quilt batting
(one 10" x 8" [25 x 20cm] piece)

Six strips of 5½" (13.7cm)-long fabric or ribbon with text written on them (any color except white)

Eight strips of 5½" (13.7cm)-long shredded paper, any color except white (or substitute ¼" (.6cm)-wide cut strips of paper)

White thread

Black thread

6" x 4" (15 x 10cm) template

INSTRUCTIONS

1. Prepare your quilt by making a sandwich of the top white cotton fabric, the quilt batting, and the bottom white fabric.

2. Lay the strips of fabric or ribbon vertically on the quilt top. arranging them at different angles.

3. Sew white zigzag stitches on the edges of each of the fabric strips through all three layers of fabric. **(A)**

4. Lay the pieces of shredded paper vertically on the quilt top, over the sewn fabric strips. Position the paper at different angles.

5. Sew straight white stitches through the middle of the paper strips through all three layers of fabric. **(B)**

6. Place the 6" x 4" (15 x 10cm) template on the quilt top to find the desired angle and placement of design.

7. To cut the quilt to size and finish the edges, refer to the "Finishing the Quilts" instructions in the "Getting Started" section on page 19. Use black thread when sewing straight and white thread for the zigzag stitches.

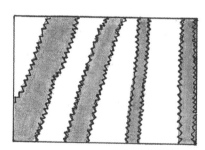

A

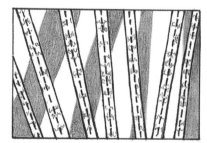

B

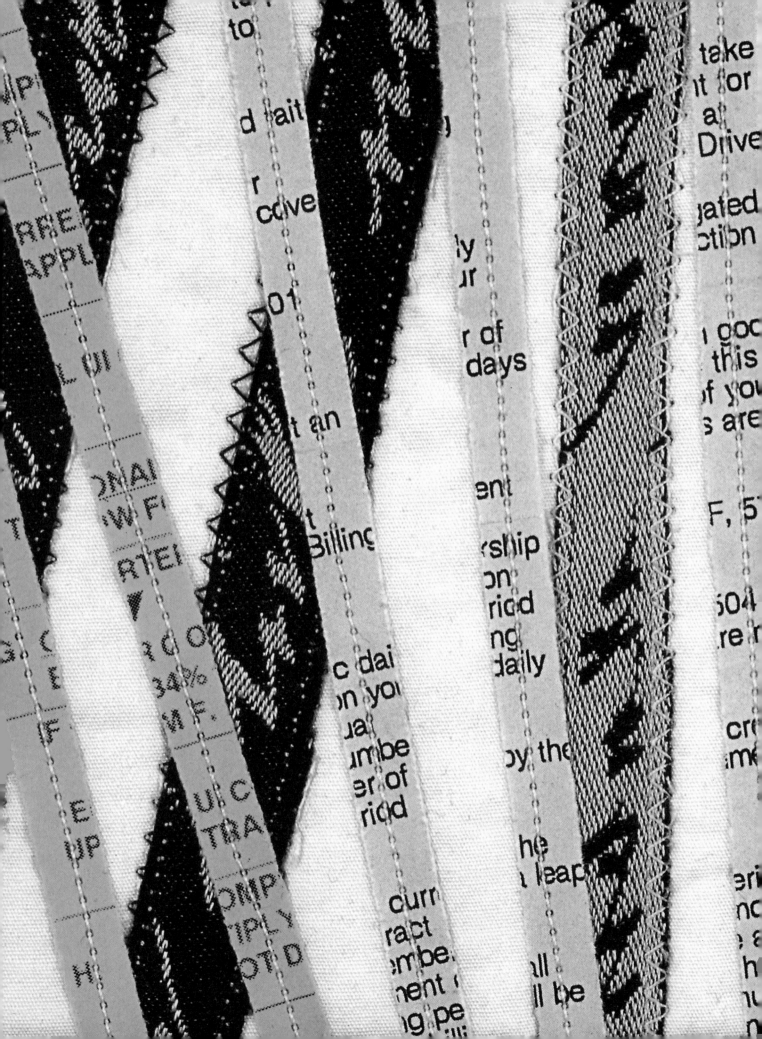

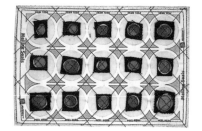

May 2002, 6" x 4" (15 x 10cm)

Dozens of sheets of used mailing labels inspired this quilt. Its logical, geometric design made the perfect foundation for a whimsical quilt made personal through the addition of thread and scraps of fabric.

Mailing Seal Leftovers

MATERIALS

White cotton fabric
(two 10" x 8" [25 x 20cm] pieces)

Quilt batting
(one 10" x 8" [25 x 20cm] piece)

One 4" x 6" (10 x 15cm) sheet of mailing seals, center round seals removed (or substitute a 4" x 6" (10 x 15cm) piece of paper with three rows of five 1" (2.5cm) circles cut out)

Fifteen ½–⅝" (1.2–1.5cm) square scraps of dark or colorful fabric (black fabric with colored dots shown)

Black thread

6" x 4" (15x10cm) template

INSTRUCTIONS

1. Prepare your quilt by making a sandwich of the top white cotton fabric, to quilt batting, and the bottom white fabric.

2. Peel the top off the backing of a mailing seal sheet and apply to the center top white fabric.

3. Place the fifteen ½–⅝" (1.2–1.5cm) square scraps of dark or colorful fabric inside the open circles. Pin in place, if desired. **(A)** Starting at one outer corner of the mailing seal sheet, sew straight black stitches diagonally through the open circles and the square scraps of fabric.

4. Repeat to sew straight black stitches thirteen more times—starting the lines at the edge of the mailing seal sheet and sewing diagonally through each open circle and over each of the ½"–⅝" (1.2–1.5cm) square scraps of fabric. The sewn stitches should create a diagonal grid across the quilt top that holds the square scraps of fabric in place. **(B)**

5. Place the 6" x 4" (15 x 10cm) template on quilt top to find the desired angle and placement of design.

6. To cut the quilt to size and finish the edges, refer to the "Finishing the Quilts" instructions in the "Getting Started" section on page 19. Use black thread when sewing straight and white thread for the zigzag stitches.

A

B

December 2002, 6" x 4" (15 x 10cm)

This striking collage looks like a delicate Victorian-era inking, but it is actually composed of a pretty blue cupcake wrapper and contrasting blue ribbon that were readily available.

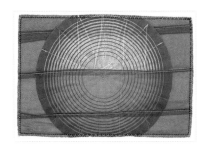

Cupcake Design

MATERIALS

White cotton fabric
(two 10" x 8" [25 x 20cm] pieces)

Quilt batting
(one 10" x 8" [25 x 20cm] piece)

Four 7" (17.5cm)-long pieces of 1½" (3.7cm)-wide sheer ribbon, color to match cupcake wrapper

One large, clean cupcake wrapper

White thread

Black thread

6" x 4" (15 x 10cm) template

INSTRUCTIONS

1. Prepare your quilt by making a sandwich of the top white cotton fabric, the quilt batting, and the bottom white fabric.

2. Place the bottom edge of the ribbon at the middle of the quilt top. Then, position two rows of ribbon horizontally on top, overlapping them slightly.

3. Sew straight white stitches as close as possible to the edges of the ribbons. **(A)**

4. Flatten and smooth the cupcake wrapper with your hands and place the top half on top of the ribbons, in the center of the quilt.

5. Starting at the top edge of the cupcake wrapper, stitch straight white stitches from the outside edge of the wrapper; stop at the center.

6. Rotate the quilt slightly and repeat to sew the stitched lines from the outer edge of the wrapper to the center, approximately every ¾" (1.9cm).

7. Do not trim the threads at the edge of the sewn wrapper; rather, let them hang 1¼"–1½" (3.1–3.7cm) loose. **(B)**

8. Add two rows of sheer ribbon, placing them horizontally over the bottom half of the wrapper. Position the top edge of one of the ribbons at the middle of the cupcake wrapper, so that it touches the edge of the ribbon that is under the wrapper. Overlap the second ribbon slightly over the first. Sew straight white stitches as close as possible to the edges of the ribbons. **(C)**

9. Place the 6" x 4" (15 x 10cm) template on the quilt top to find the desired angle and placement of design.

10. To cut the quilt to size and finish the edges, refer to the "Finishing the Quilts" instructions in the "Getting Started" section on page 19. Use black thread when sewing straight and white thread for the zigzag stitches.

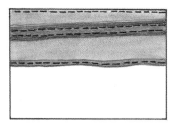

A

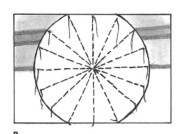

B

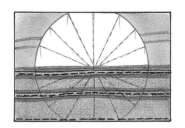

C

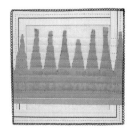

August 2003, 6" x 6" (15 x 15cm)

Newspapers have a tendency to tear in transit. Instead of scrapping a shredded page from my morning read, I took the deconstructed paper and resuscitated it with a photograph frame and multiple lines of stitching.

Problem

Newspaper

MATERIALS

White cotton fabric
(two 10" x 10" [25 x 25cm] pieces)

Quilt batting
(one 10" x 10" [25 x 25cm] piece)

Paper frame from an old photograph (or substitute a piece of heavy paper cut like a frame or template)
Note: See the instructions for cutting a template in the "How to Use a Design Template" in the "Getting Started" section on page 19.

Torn 7" x 4" (17.5 x 10cm) newspaper (or off-white paper)

White thread

Black thread

6" x 6" (15 x 15cm) template

INSTRUCTIONS

1. Prepare your quilt by making a sandwich of the top white cotton fabric, the quilt batting, and the bottom white fabric.

2. Cut a paper frame diagonally in half to yield two corners or two right angles.

3. Place one of the two corners or right angles on the white quilt top, near the top left edge of the white top fabric.

4. Place the second corner on the white quilt top, near the bottom right edge of the white top fabric; overlap the cut ends of the second frame with the cut ends of the first frame. The outer edge of the frame "square" should measure 6" (15cm) across.

5. Sew white stitches on all four sides of the paper frame, ½" (1.2cm) from the inside edge of the frame. **(A)**

6. Position the torn newspaper horizontally on the white top fabric so it covers part of the left and right edges of the sewn paper frame.

7. Sew horizontal white lines across the newspaper, starting at the left bottom edge of the paper, and ending at the bottom right side.

8. Repeat to sew eight additional horizontal white lines across the newspaper every ³⁄₈" (.9cm) until the newspaper is totally stitched in place. **(B)**

9. Place the 6" x 6" (15 x 15cm) template on quilt top to find the desired angle and placement of design.

10. To cut the quilt to size and finish the edges, refer to the "Finishing the Quilts" instructions in the "Getting Started" section on page 19. Use black thread when sewing straight and zigzag stitches.

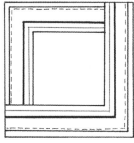

A

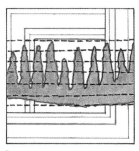

B

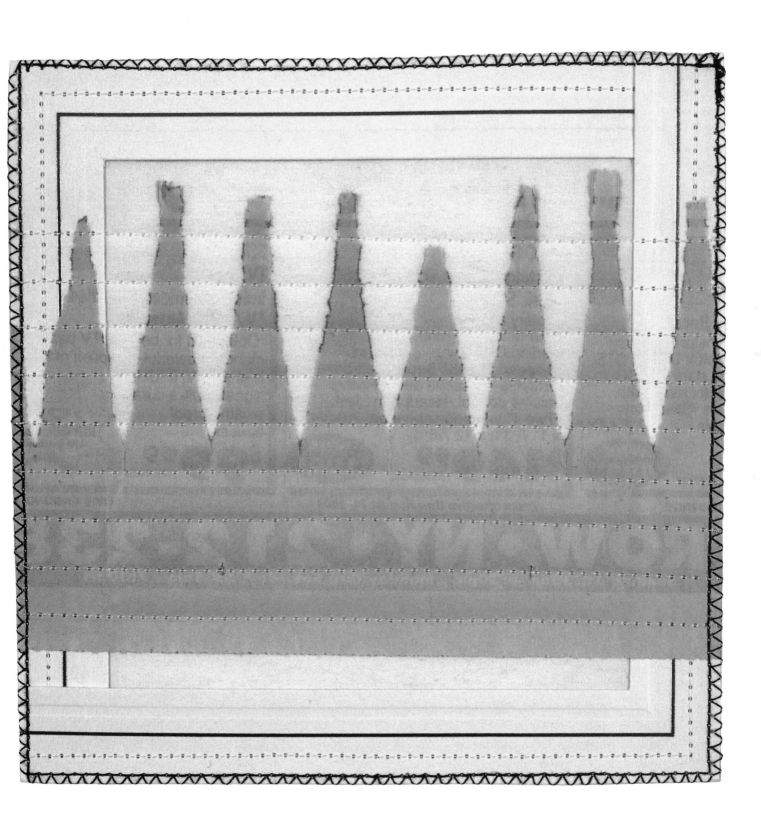

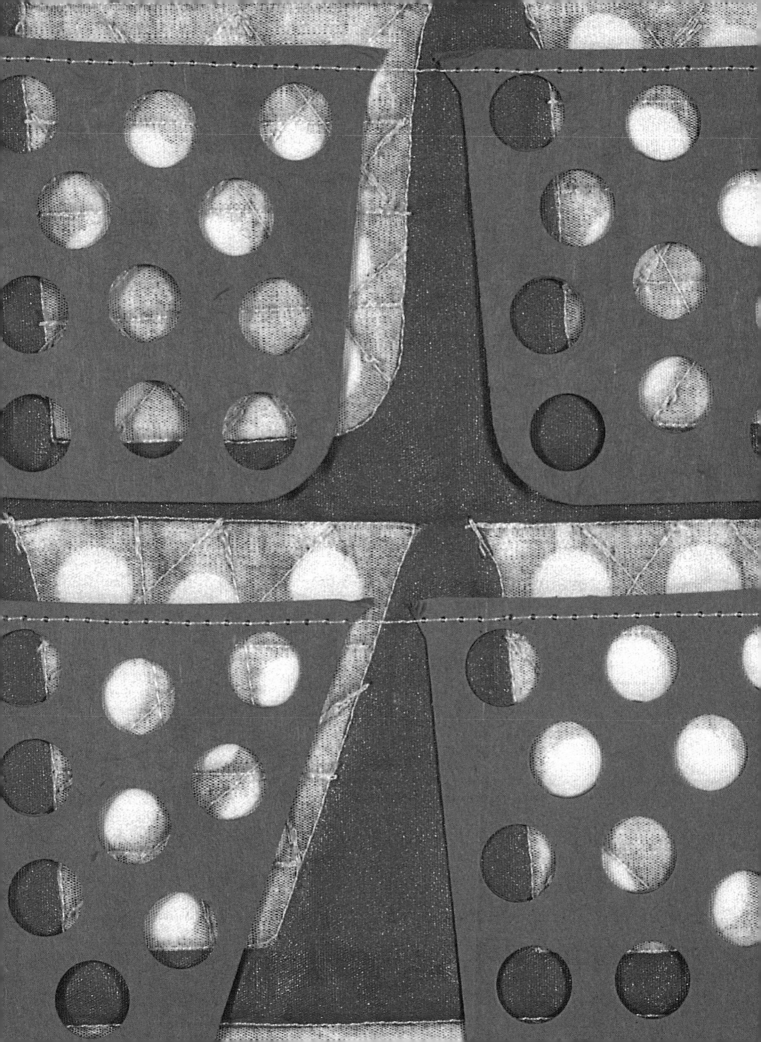

The hot beverage sleeve that enveloped my latte cup had a surprisingly decorative pattern on its inner band. I not only made a crayon rubbing of its texture but also stitched it to my quilt.

Off-Center Design

MATERIALS

White cotton fabric
(two 10" x 10" [25 x 25cm] pieces)

Quilt batting
(one 10" x 10" [25 x 25cm] piece)

Cardboard coffee cup sleeve (or substitute four 2"–2½" (5–6.2cm) pieces of cardboard with cut or punched holes)

Brown crayon

Metallic brown fabric paint

White thread

Black thread

Iron and ironing board

6" x 6" (15 x 15cm) template

INSTRUCTIONS

1. Place the cardboard coffee cup sleeve or hole-punched cardboard pieces on a flat surface, and place one of the 10" x 10" (25 x 25cm) pieces of white cotton fabric on top of the cardboard pieces.

2. Using the long end of a large, wide brown crayon, rub gently across the fabric, taking care to transfer the texture of the object. Rub lightly at first, trying not to snag the fabric. Press harder as you rub, trying to pick up the texture. Remove the fabric from your work surface and place it on an ironing board. (A)

3. Cover the fabric with a paper towel. Iron at the appropriate setting for your fabric (with steam setting off) until the crayon has melted into the fabric. This should take less than one minute.

4. Prepare your quilt by making a sandwich of the top white cotton fabric, the quilt batting, and the bottom white fabric.

5. Sew straight white stitches around the outside of the crayon rubbing design, and then sew random straight white stitches around the inside of the crayon rubbing design. (B)

6. Apply metallic brown fabric paint onto the remaining white top fabric around the crayon rubbing (refer to the "Surface Design" chapter on page 85). Let dry.

7. Position the cardboard coffee cup sleeve or hole-punched cardboard pieces off center from the crayon rubbings of the same shapes.

8. Sew horizontally across the top edges of the hole-punched cardboard pieces to attach them to the quilt. (C)

9. Place the 6" x 6" (15 x 15cm) template on the quilt top to find the desired angle and placement of design.

10. To cut the quilt to size and finish the edges, refer to the "Finishing the Quilts" instructions in the "Getting Started" section on page 19. Use black thread when sewing straight and zigzag stitches.

A

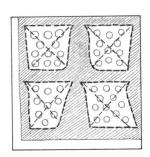

B

C

December 2003, 6" x 6" (15 x 15cm)

Like a sun rising over an open expanse (or the yolk of an egg, depending on your perspective), this design is a simple paean to the small pleasures in life.

Sunny-Side Up

MATERIALS

White cotton fabric
(two 10" x 10" [25 x 25cm] pieces)

Quilt batting
(one 10" x 10" [25 x 25cm] piece)

One paper potato bag with netting window (4½" x 6½" [11.2 x 16.2cm])

One 2" (5cm) orange fabric circle on a square white background (or substitute one 2" orange fabric circle)

One 5½" (13.7cm)-long piece of 1" (2.5cm)-wide green ribbon

One 7" (17.5cm)-long piece of 1" (2.5)-wide red and pink patterned fabric (or substitute ribbon)

White thread

Black thread

6" x 6" (15 x 15cm) template

INSTRUCTIONS

1. Prepare your quilt by making a sandwich of the top white cotton fabric, the quilt batting, and the bottom white fabric.

2. Position the 2" (5cm) orange circle in the center of the top white fabric and sew straight white stitches around the edges. (A)

3. Place the cut paper potato bag in the center of the quilt top, positioning the net window over the orange circle.

4. Sew straight white stitches ⅛" (.3cm) from all four edges of the paper bag, and then sew straight white stitches ⅛" (.3cm) from the paper edge of the net window. (B)

5. Bevel both of the edges of the 5" (12.5cm)-long piece of ribbon 45 degrees so the inner edge of the ribbon is 4" (10cm) long and the outer edge is 5½" (13.7cm).

6. Position the green ribbon horizontally over the paper bag, with the 4" (10cm) end side up, placing it 1¼" (3.1cm) below the bottom edge of the orange circle. Sew the green ribbon in place using straight white stitches.

7. Place the red and pink patterned fabric horizontally over the paper bag, measuring 1¼" (3.1cm) above the top edge of the orange circle. Sew straight white stitches close to the edges of the red and pink patterned fabric. (C)

8. Place the 6" x 6" (15 x 15cm) template on the quilt top to find the desired angle and placement of design.

9. To cut the quilt to size and finish the edges, refer to the "Finishing the Quilts" instructions in the "Getting Started" section on page 19. Use black thread when sewing straight and zigzag stitches.

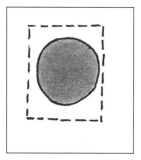

A

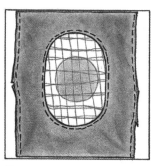

B

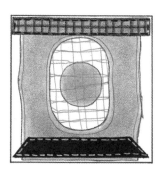

C

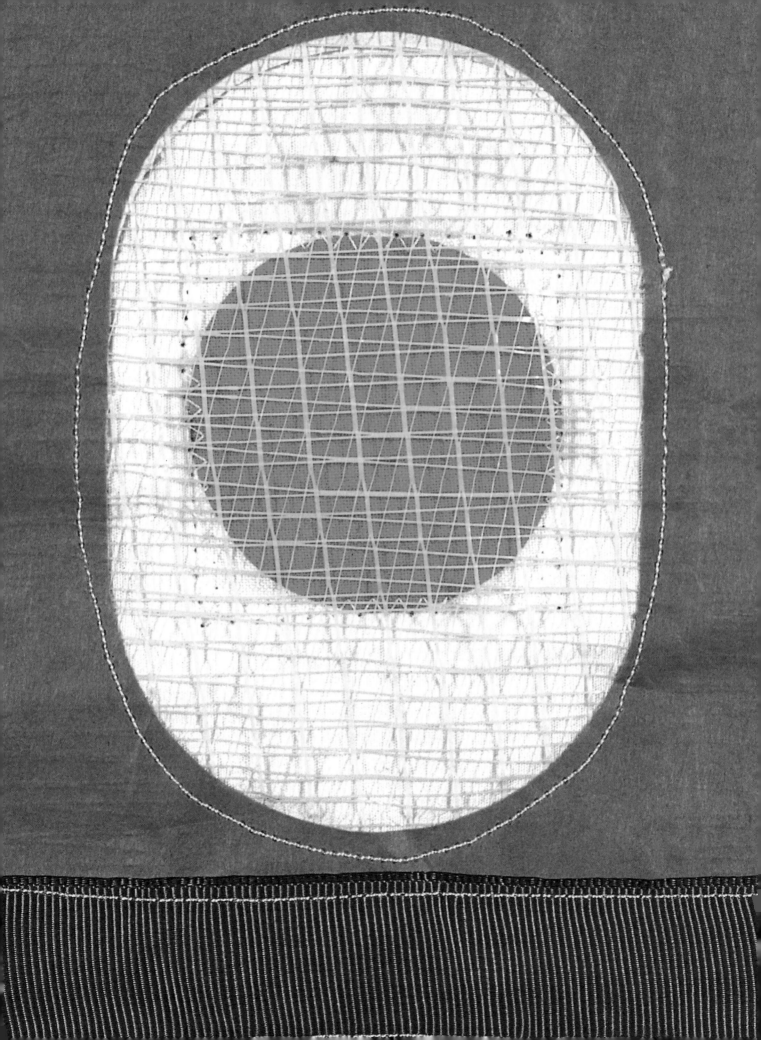

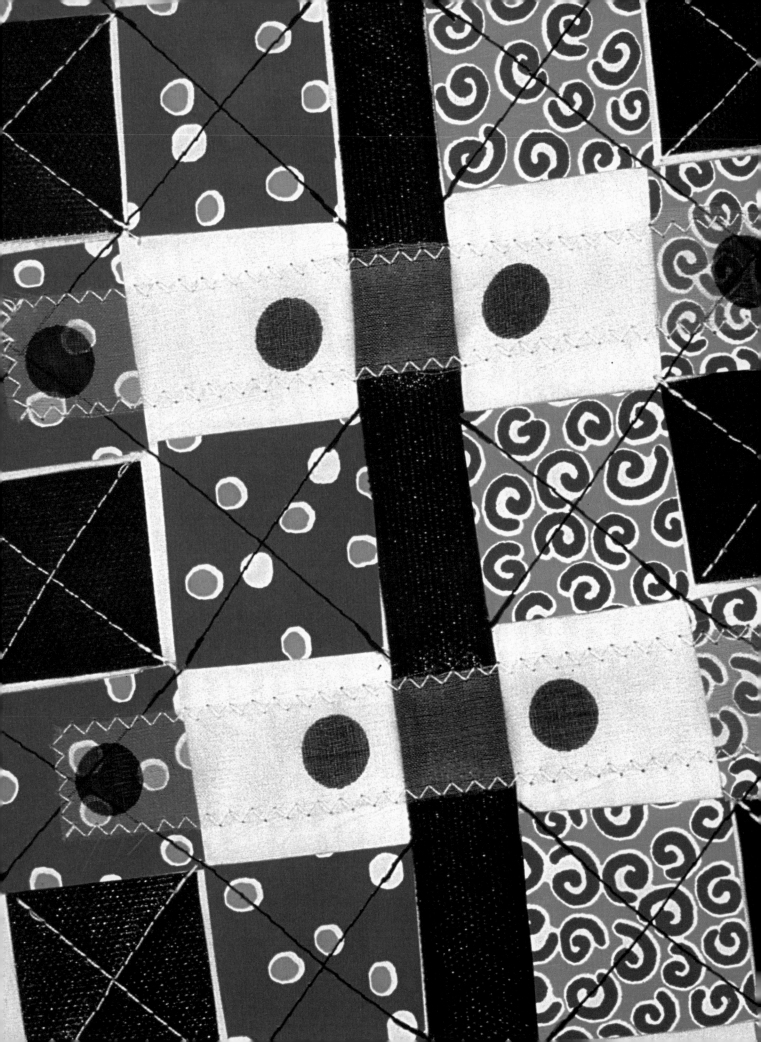

Sometimes a quilt is just a quilt. I couldn't resist making this "patchwork quilt" using recycled gift wrap on a whole-cloth quilt.

Recycled Patchwork

MATERIALS

White cotton fabric
(two 10" x 11" [25 x 27.5cm] pieces)

Quilt batting
(one 10" x 11" [25 x 27.5cm] piece)

Six 1¼"–1½" (3.1–3.7cm) square pieces of landscape fabric (or substitute black paper)

Ten 1¼"–1½" (3.1–3.7cm) square pieces of wrapping paper

One ¾" x 8" (1.8 x 20cm) strip of landscape fabric (or substitute black paper)

Two ¾" x 5" (1.8 x 12.5cm) strips of sheer dotted fabric (or substitute any sheer fabric)

White thread

Black thread

6" x 7" (15 x 17.5cm) template

INSTRUCTIONS

1. Prepare your quilt by making a sandwich of the top white cotton fabric, the quilt batting, and the bottom white fabric.

2. Place the strip of landscape fabric vertically on the quilt top. Sew straight black stitches close to the edges of the strip of landscape fabric. **(A)**

3. Create a patchwork design using the ten pieces of wrapping paper and the six pieces of landscape fabric. Leave four square spaces blank.

4. Sew black straight stitches in an *"x"* across each piece of wrapping paper, using the stitching as a design element.

5. Sew white straight stitches in an *"x"* across each piece of landscape fabric. **(B)**

6. Position one piece of sheer dotted fabric horizontally across the upper row with two white spaces.

7. Position the second piece of sheer dotted fabric horizontally across the lower row with two white spaces.

8. Sew white straight stitches along all four edges of both strips of sheer dotted fabric. **(C)**

9. Place the 6" x 7" (15 x 17.5cm) template on the quilt top to find the desired angle and placement of design.

10. To cut the quilt to size and finish the edges, refer to the "Finishing the Quilts" instructions in the "Getting Started" section on page 19. Use black thread when sewing straight and zigzag stitches.

A

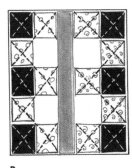

B

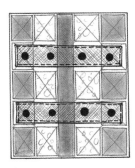

C

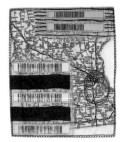

August 2004, 6" x 7" (15 x 17.5cm)

The journey of raising a child and then sending him off to school was an emotional experience. The variety of feelings and places it took me are reflected in the multiple media elements included in this quilt's design.

College Drop-Off

MATERIALS

White cotton fabric
(two 10" x 11" [25 x 27.5cm] pieces)

Quilt batting
(one 10" x 11" [25 x 27.5cm] piece)

One 6½" (16.2cm) square section of paper map

Six bar codes from used boarding passes (or substitute any thin bar codes or fabric with thin vertical stripes)

One 4½" x 1½" (11.2 x 3.7cm) piece of sheer fabric with thin stripes

One 4" x 4½" (10 x 11.2cm) piece of sheer fabric with wide stripes

White thread

Red thread

Black thread

6" x 7" (15 x 17.5cm) template

INSTRUCTIONS

1. Prepare your quilt by making a sandwich of the top white cotton fabric, the quilt batting, and the bottom white fabric.

2. Place the map in the center of the top white quilt fabric. Sew straight white stitches around the edges of the map. (A)

3. Sew the five bar codes from used boarding passes onto the quilt top.

4. Cut one 4½" x 1½" (11.2 x 3.7cm) piece of sheer fabric with thin stripes. (The striped fabric should be a larger size than the bar codes. Adjust the fabric size if needed.)

5. Cut one 4" x 4½" (10.2 x 11.4cm) piece of sheer fabric with wide stripes. (The striped fabric should be a larger size than the bar codes. Adjust the fabric size if needed.)

6. Position the 4" x 4½" (10.2 x 11.4cm) piece of sheer fabric with wide stripes at the lower left corner of the quilt on top of the map.

Place three of the bar codes on top of the sheer fabric with stripes, and stitch the bar codes and striped fabric to quilt top using white thread.

7. Place two of the bar codes on top of the sheer striped fabric, and stitch the fabric and bar codes to the quilt top using white thread. (B)

8. Select the area to highlight on the map and stitch red circles around the area, sewing round and round to create four circles. (C)

9. Place the 6" x 7" (15 x 17.5cm) template on the quilt top to find the desired angle and placement of design.

10. To cut the quilt to size and finish the edges, refer to the "Finishing the Quilts" instructions in the "Getting Started" section on page 19. Use black thread when sewing straight and zigzag stitches.

A

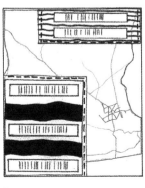

B

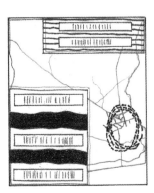

C

May 2004, 6" x 7" (15 x 17.5cm)

Delicate paper flowers recalled the vulnerability of springtime for me. Fabric leaves completed the feeling of being completely enveloped by nature.

Tissue Collage

MATERIALS

White cotton fabric
(two 10" x 11" [25 x 27.5cm] pieces)

Quilt batting
(one 10" x 11" [25 x 27.5cm] piece)

One 2⅛" x 7" (5.3 x 17.5cm) piece of a decorative tissue, with tulips or other flowers (or substitute fabric)

Four 1½" x 2½" (3.7 x 6.2cm) or smaller pieces of black and white leaf-print fabric

One orange-colored fabric flower, cut in half

White thread

Black thread

6" x 7" (15 x 17.5cm) template

INSTRUCTIONS

1. Prepare your quilt by making a sandwich of the top white cotton fabric, the quilt batting, and the bottom white fabric.

2. Place the piece of decorative tissue vertically on the top white fabric, slightly left of the center.

3. Sew straight black stitches close to the edges of the decorative tissue. **(A)**

4. Create a collage using the pieces of black and white leaf fabric by placing them near the bottom of the quilt top, next to the tissue piece.

5. Sew the leaf fabric pieces in place using black zigzag stitches around the edges of the fabric.

6. Sew black straight stitches over the zigzag stitches completed in the previous step.

7. Position the two halves of the cut orange flower on the upper edges of white top fabric, 1"–1½" (2.5–3.7cm) from the top of the quilt.

8. Sew the flower pieces in place using orange zigzag stitches around the edges of both flowers. **(B)**

9. Place the 6" x 7" (15 x 17.5cm) template on the quilt top to find the desired angle and placement of design.

10. To cut the quilt to size and finish the edges, refer to the "Finishing the Quilts" instructions in the "Getting Started" section on page 19. Use black thread when sewing straight and zigzag stitches.

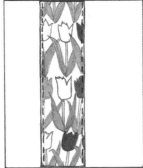

A

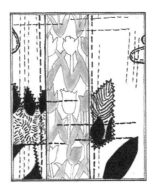

B

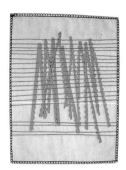

September 2005, 6" x 8" (15 x 20cm)

This quilt reflects my husband's campaign for local public office. The folded papers, which are stitched with fuschia thread, are the scraps of the thank-you letters he sent for donations.

Folded Stitched Paper

MATERIALS

White cotton fabric
(two 10" x 12" [25 x 30cm] pieces)

Quilt batting
(one 10" x 12" [25 x 30cm] piece)

Nine 8½" (21.2cm)-tall, ³⁄₁₆" (.7cm)-wide strips of gray card stock (shown cut with one wavy edge)

Fuchsia thread

Black thread

6" x 8" (15 x 20cm) template

INSTRUCTIONS

1. Prepare your quilt by making a sandwich of the top white cotton fabric, the quilt batting, and the bottom white fabric.

2. Randomly fold one of the gray card stock strips in half, and place in the center of the quilt top fabric. Sew two random lines of straight fuchsia stitches horizontally across the white fabric, sewing over the folded gray strip. Start at one side of the fabric and stitch across to the other side. **(A)**

3. Repeat eight more times, randomly folding the strips and sewing fuchsia lines over the new and previously attached strips. Add extra rows of stitching, if desired, to hold down the ends of all the strips.

4. Place the 6" x 8" (15 x 20cm) template on the quilt top to find the desired angle and placement of design.

5. To cut the quilt to size and finish the edges, refer to the "Finishing the Quilts" instructions in the "Getting Started" section on page 19. Use black thread when sewing straight and zigzag stitches.

A

June 2003, 6" x 6" (15 x 15cm)

Water lilies have a surprisingly hardy feel to them, despite their delicate appearance in Impressionist oil paintings. Using thick photo paper, I mimicked the texture of the natural object and added scrap fabric flowers to complete the collage.

Water Lily Collage

MATERIALS

White cotton fabric
(two 10" x 10" [25 x 25cm] pieces)

Quilt batting (one 10" x 10"
[25 x 25cm] piece)

One 3½" x 4" (8.7 x 10cm) flower, digitally printed on regular paper (or substitute a flower cut from a magazine or a greeting card)

Scraps of flowered fabric

White thread

Black thread

6" x 6" (15 x 15cm) template

INSTRUCTIONS

1. Prepare your quilt by making a sandwich of the top white cotton fabric, the quilt batting, and the bottom white fabric.

2. Make a collage with assorted scraps of flowered fabric on the quilt top. Leave the center section of the white fabric empty. Stitch the flower collage to the white fabric, sewing random straight white stitches. Sew as desired, following lines or patterns of interest. Set aside a few pieces of flowered fabric for later.

3. Cut out the paper flower image. Place the paper flower in the center white section of the quilt, over the fabric collage. Stitch straight white stitches ⅛" (.3cm) from the outer edges of the paper flower.

4. Position a few more fabric flowers on the quilt, slightly overlapping. Stitch the additional flowers to the collage, sewing straight white or black stitches.

5. Starting at the center of the flower, stitch white straight stitches over the stamens. Sew approximately 1"–1¼" (2.5–3.1cm) out toward the edges, and then back to the center. Pivot the needle and stitch seven additional lines.

6. Place the 6" x 6" (15 x 15cm) template on the quilt top to find the desired angle and placement of design.

7. To cut the quilt to size and finish the edges, refer to the "Finishing the Quilts" instructions in the "Getting Started" section on page 19. Use black thread when sewing straight and zigzag stitches.

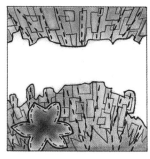

A

B

June 2000, 8" x 7" (20 x 17cm)

Although this quilt is similar to one I made while in London (pages 48–49), it is assembled in a much different manner, using a mixed-media approach. Before leaving for my trip, I sewed two pieces of netting together to make nine pockets, collecting small objects along the way and then hand stitching the pockets closed.

Amsterdam & Paris Vacation

MATERIALS

White cotton fabric
(two 12" x 11" [30 x 27.5cm] pieces)

Quilt batting
(one 12" x 11" [30 x 27.5cm] piece)

Two 7" x 7" (17.5 x 17.5cm) pieces of black fabric netting

Small flat objects collected on a trip (tickets, tourist brochures, coins, etc.)

Black thread

White thread

Hand sewing needle

Scissors

8" x 7" (20 x 17.5cm) template

INSTRUCTIONS

1. Before traveling, place one piece of black fabric netting on top of the other. Stitch them together with straight black stitches, from the top to the bottom of the netting, 2½" (6.2cm) from the two side edges. Sew a straight line from one side of the netting to the other side, 2½" (6.2cm) from the top and the bottom edge. The end result will be a grid of three rows and three columns of 2" (5cm) squares. (A)

2. Stitch ½" (1.3cm) from all four of the edges of the netting, along the outside edges of the grid, to complete the 2" (5cm) squares.

3. Trim ¼" (.6cm) off all four of the edges of the netting, so the netting measures 6½" (16.2cm) on all sides.

4. Carefully cut an opening at the top section of each of the 2" (5cm) squares, so the squares now become nine miniature pockets. (B)

5. While traveling, fill each pocket with small flat objects from the trip, such as ticket stubs, tourist brochures, receipts, small or folded postcards, coins, etc.

6. Once the pockets are full, carefully hand-stitch each one closed with black thread.

7. Prepare your quilt by making a sandwich of the top white cotton fabric, the quilt batting, and the bottom white fabric.

8. Position the finished netting square in the center of the quilt top. Pin in place if desired.

9. Hand stitch the netting square to the top white fabric, sewing a black "x" at the corner of each 2" (5cm) square.

10. Sewing by hand and using black thread, stitch a straight line ⅛" (.3cm) around the outside edge of the netting square. (C)

11. After traveling, place the 8" x 7" (20 x 17.5cm) template on the quilt top to find the desired angle and placement of design.

12. To cut the quilt to size and finish the edges, refer to the "Finishing the Quilts" instructions in the "Getting Started" section on page 19. Use white thread when sewing straight and zigzag stitches.

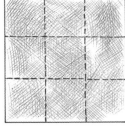

A

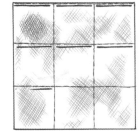

B

C

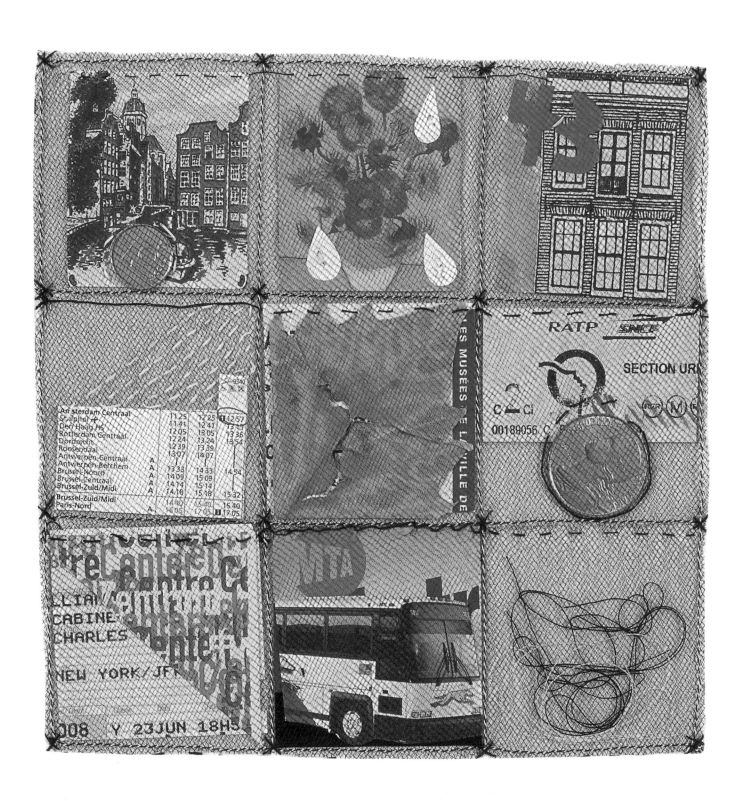

Surface Design

Surface design can be intimidating if you do not have extensive experience working with fabric, but it isn't as daunting as it might seem. Many people assume surface design involves complex techniques such as screen printing, resist/discharge (batiking and fabric bleaching), and digital printing. Yet in truth, many surface design techniques are accessible to beginners. Using minimal supplies and inexpensive equipment, beginner surface designers can experiment with crayon rubbing, fabric painting, and hand-stamping (using pencil erasers or the end of a paintbrush).

Crayon Rubbings

When you were a child, did you ever make gravestone rubbings? If you did, you probably remember placing a piece of paper over a gravestone, then rubbing a big crayon over the surface to copy the engraved text or design. I grew up in a New England town with gravestones dating back to the early 1700s; as children, we made rubbings to help decode the time-worn and almost illegible dates and names on the stones. This same basic technique can be used to create textures on fabric. To make the design permanent, simply iron it in place. To get started, you'll need the following:

- Fabric
- One large, wide crayon
- Masking tape
- Flat, textured items, such as cardboard from children's games or various types of netting
- Paper towels
- Iron and ironing board (Note: Use the iron with the steam setting turned off.)

Start by placing the textured object flat on the table. Tape it in place to prevent slippage. Place the fabric over the textured object, taping the fabric in place, if necessary.

Gently rub the end of the large, wide crayon across the fabric, taking care to capture the texture of the object on the fabric. Rub lightly at first, and be careful not to snag the fabric. Press harder as you continue rubbing, picking up the objects texture, and stop when you like the results. Remove the fabric from the textured item, place a paper towel over the rubbing, and then iron the fabric with the steam setting off. (Be sure to adjust the heat setting to the appropriate temperature for your fabric.) Iron the piece until the crayon has melted (this should take less than a minute). After ironing, the crayon pattern will be permanently embedded in your fabric, and you can move on to the next step of your project.

Working with Fabric

Decorating the surface of fabric with paint is another simple technique that can produce beautiful and unique surface designs. If you have ever painted a wall in your home, then you have more than enough painting experience to use fabric paint. You'll need the following items:

- Fabric
- Fabric paint
- Deveral small, inexpensive paintbrushes
- A cup or jar of water for rinsing the brush
- Rags or paper towels for cleaning up spills
- An iron with the steam setting turned off

A few words of caution about using fabric paint: Wear an apron or old clothing while working, as the paint will leave a permanent mark on any fabric it touches. Most fabric paint labels imply that the paint isn't permanently set until it has been ironed, but I've found that most fabric paints are permanent on contact.

The instructions in this book call for transparent fabric paint, unless opaque fabric paint is specified. I prefer Jacquard Textile Colors, but you can use PROfab Transparent Textile Paint by ProChem or Setacolor Fabric Paint by Pebeo. If you like opaque or metallic fabric paints, I suggest Lumiere and Neopaque, PROfab Opaque Paint, PERObrite Pearlescent Textile Paint, or Setacolor Opaque & Pearlescent Colors.

Previous page: To create the look of stained glass, sew first, then paint right up to the stitching, leaving a small white border between the paint and the stitches.

Your first experiment with fabric paint might be painting a picture or a design on fabric. Another variation on this simple technique is shading; for subtle color, paint the surface lightly, using very little fabric paint on your brush, or vary your technique by applying smaller amounts of paint in some areas and more saturated color in others.

Sew First, Then Paint

There is no reason why you can't apply paint to your quilt after it has been sewn. I like to stitch different shapes or lines onto a white fabric quilt, then apply paint to the quilt top. Painting different distances from the stitched line will change the effects you create.

If you feel more comfortable working within the lines of a design, try painting right up to the stitching. Doing so creates a solid shape with a nice outline. You might also try painting with the same color as your thread, or stitch with black thread and fill in the shape with a contrasting color of paint.

To create a stained glass effect, you will need to create a thicker line separating the sections of your image (mimicking the leading used in traditional stained glass). By matching the fabric color and the thread color and painting close to your sewn design without touching the stitching, you will create a thicker outline of your shape.

You can also combine fabric painting with other surface design techniques for more varied effects. After creating a crayon rubbing on fabric, for instance, you might also try painting the rubbing to highlight or even partially obscure the design.

Varying the amount of paint you apply to your fabric can create different effects.

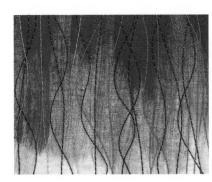

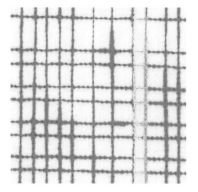

Fabric paint seeps to the quilt front along the stitching lines if you paint on the back of the quilt first. The result is a delicate pattern.

Experiment with applying the fabric paint using a pencil eraser. Simply dip the eraser lightly in fabric paint, and then press or stamp the painted eraser on the fabric to create a small, solid circle. Similarly, you can dip the end of a paintbrush handle in paint and pressing it onto the fabric, create a smaller circle depending on the thickness of the handle.

When painting near stitching on the front of a quilt one day, I noticed that sometimes the fabric paint seeped from the front of the quilt to the quilt back. At first I was unhappy about this, but then I was able to use it as a design technique. Why not paint the back of a quilt, using the reverse design as a pattern?

If you want to try this technique, I recommend sewing your design first on the front of the fabric, and then painting over the stitching on the back. To do this, pour some fabric paint in an old bowl or paper cup. (Only use vessels that are no longer being used for eating or cooking. It's always important to keep kitchen and art supplies separated as some art supplies contain chemicals that are toxic if ingested.) After you have poured a small amount of paint, add a little water to thin it slightly. Paint on the quilt back and allow the pigment to seep through to the front. If the color does not seep through, add water incrementally to your original mixture, painting over the area again. It may take a half-hour or so to complete the entire process, as the initial saturation may appear lighter than the color that will eventually seep through the fabric.

Marking Your Quilts

If you want to document the techniques you used to decorate your quilt or to add thoughts and dates, use a permanent marker to make notes on the quilt's back. I like to note the date, the technique, and the influenceds on me at the time, but you should match your entry to your interests. You might also use your permanent marker to highlight an area on the quilt's front, much as you would on a piece of paper.

As you can see from the varying surface design techniques discussed here, the possibilities for variation are endless—so follow your heart and let your art speak for itself.

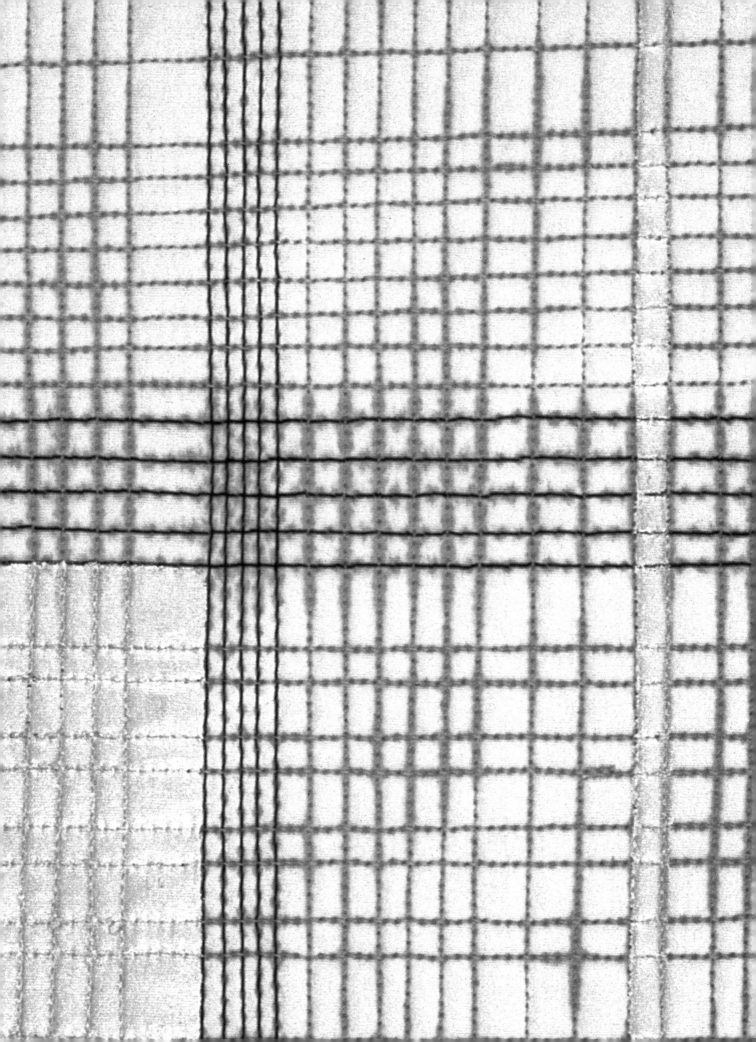

April 2000, 8" x 7" (20 x 17.5cm)

It feels as if spring has finally arrived in Massachusetts when the forsythia blooms. This quilt captures the beauty of the mounds of yellow flowers that blanket my neighborhood, using sewn lines and fabric paint.

MATERIALS

White cotton fabric
(two 12" x 11" [30 x 27.5cm] pieces)

Quilt batting
(one 12" x 11" [30 x 27.5cm] piece)

One pencil with an eraser

Yellow fabric paint

Brown fabric paint

Small paintbrush

Laundry pen or
permanent marker

Brown thread

Blue thread

White thread

7" x 7" (20 x 17.5cm) template

Forsythia

INSTRUCTIONS

1. Prepare your quilt by making a sandwich of the top white cotton fabric, the quilt batting, and the bottom white fabric.

2. Stitch the forsythia bushes with brown thread using straight stitches, starting your sewing near the bottom of the white quilt top, and sew toward the top of the quilt. Sew slightly curved lines, so the branches "bend" as little or as much as you'd like.

3. Sew up to four branches (again, using stitched brown lines) out of each trunk-like base from step 2 and leave some bushes with single branches. Randomly place the bushes ³⁄₈"–³⁄₄" (.9–1.8cm) apart. Sew in slightly curved lines so the branches "bend." **(A)**

4. Dip the eraser end of a pencil in the yellow fabric paint. Stamp the paint-covered eraser into the fabric along the edges of the stitched brown branches. Allow the paint to dry.

5. To give the appearance that the flowers are attached to the branch, draw "v" shapes with a laundry pen or

permanent marker. Start drawing the "v" about ¹⁄₈" (.3cm) from each stitched branch, so the point of the "v" touches the stitching. **(B)**

6. Approximately 1" (2.5cm) up from the bottom of the quilt, stitch a wavy line using brown thread to represent the ground beneath the bushes. Using brown fabric paint, paint the "ground."

7. Starting slightly above the stitched painted "ground," sew straight blue stitches from one side of the quilt top to the other side. Repeat the blue stitched lines every ¹⁄₂" (1.2cm) until you have stitched 6¹⁄₂" (16.2cm) lines above the "ground." Don't worry if you stitch over the forsythia. **(C)**

8. Place the 8" x 7" (20 x 17.5cm) template on the quilt top to find the desired angle and placement of design.

9. To cut the quilt to size and finish edges, refer to the "Finishing the Quilts" instructions in the "Getting Started" section on page 19. Use white thread when sewing straight and zigzag stitches.

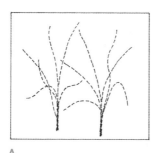

A

B

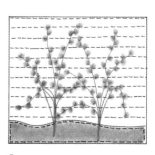

C

June 2001, 4" x 6" (10 x 15cm)

When the bloom is past its peak, and the flowers are dried out, allium flowers look like aliens from outer space. I re-created the flowers using thread and fabric paint.

Alien Allium Flowers

MATERIALS

White cotton fabric
(two 8" x 10" [20 x 25cm] pieces)

Quilt batting
(one 8" x 10" [20 x 25cm] piece)

Opaque green fabric paint

Dark yellow fabric paint

Pencil with an eraser

Small paintbrush

Dark yellow thread

Green thread

White thread

4" x 6" (10 x 15cm) template

INSTRUCTIONS

1. Prepare your quilt by making a sandwich of the top white cotton fabric, the quilt batting, and the bottom white fabric.

2. To create the first "stem," start sewing 1" (2.5cm) to the right of the center of the quilt. At the bottom edge of the white fabric quilt top, sew dark yellow thread straight stitches 3½" (8.7cm) toward the quilt top. Then turn the quilt 180 degrees to stitch back to the bottom of the quilt, ending about ¼"–⅜" (.6–.9cm) to the left of where you started. You will now have a tall upside-down "v."

3. To create the second "stem," start sewing 1¾" (4.3cm) to the left of the first stitched area. At the bottom edge of the white fabric quilt top, sew dark yellow thread straight stitches 5½" (13.7cm) toward the quilt top. Then turn the quilt 180 degrees to stitch back to the bottom of the quilt, about ¼"–⅜" (.5–.9cm) to the left from when you first started sewing. You will now have a second tall upside-down "v."

4. Using a thin paintbrush, paint the two "stems" with dark yellow fabric paint. Allow to dry. **(A)**

5. Using green thread, stitch from the top of the "V"-shaped right stem, approximately 1"–1½" (2.5–3.7cm) out, and back over the stitches you just sewed, ending at the top of the "v"-shaped "stem." Pivot the quilt and stitch again several times. The end result should look similar to bicycle spokes.

6. Using green thread, stitch from the top of the "V"-shaped left stem, approximately 1"–1½" (2.5–3.7cm) out, and back over the stitches you just sewed, ending at the top of the "v" shaped "stem." Pivot the quilt and stitch again repeatedly.

7. Using the eraser end of a pencil, dip the eraser lightly in opaque green fabric paint. Stamp the paint onto the fabric along the edges of the stitched green "spokes." Allow to dry. **(B)**

8. Place the 4" x 6" (10 x 15cm) template on the quilt top to find the desired angle and placement of design.

9. To cut the quilt to size and finish the edges, refer to the "Finishing the Quilts" instructions in the "Getting Started" section on page 19. Use black thread when sewing straight and white thread for the zigzag stitches.

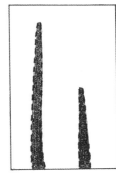

A

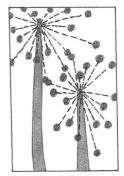

B

February 2003, 6" x 6" (15 x 15cm)

Beauty may be hell, but finding the perfect color hair dye is a fate even the devil could have never imagined. This quilt is a paean to finding the proverbial glass slipper (and getting a few grays while doing so).

Hair Dye?

MATERIALS

White cotton fabric
(two 10" x 10" [25 x 25cm] pieces)

Quilt batting
(one 10" x 10" [25 x 25cm] piece)

Brown fabric paint

Small paintbrush

Gray thread

Brown thread

Purple thread

White thread

6" x 6" (15 x 15cm) template

INSTRUCTIONS

1. Brush brown fabric paint on one 10" x 10" (25 x 25cm) piece of white cotton fabric. The paint should saturate the top of the fabric, but be lightly brushed near the bottom of the fabric, with no paint at the very bottom. Allow to dry. **(A)**

2. Prepare your quilt by making a sandwich of the top painted cotton fabric, the quilt batting, and the bottom white fabric.

3. Stitch twenty-two random wavy brown lines, starting at the brownest part of the quilt (at the top) that reach to the white section at the bottom. The wavy lines should resemble hair.

4. Stitch a few random wavy gray lines, again starting at the top of the quilt, that reach to the white section at the bottom.

5. Stitch a few random wavy purple lines in the same way. **(B)**

6. Place the 6" x 6" (15 x 15cm) template on the quilt top to find the desired angle and placement of design.

7. To cut the quilt to size and finish the edges, refer to the "Finishing the Quilts" instructions in the "Getting Started" section on page 19. Use white thread when sewing straight and zigzag stitches.

A

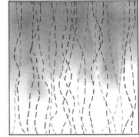

B

June 2004, 6" x 7" (15 x 17.5cm)

Upon finishing a small painted quilt, I noticed the paint had seeped through both the stitching and quilt batting and was showing on the quilt back, creating a pleasing, light pattern to decorate. It's proof positive a mistake is never really a setback when you're making your quilts!

Accidentally on Purpose

MATERIALS

White cotton fabric
(two 10" x 11" [25 x 27.5cm] pieces)

Quilt batting
(one 10" x 11" [25 x 27.5cm] piece)

Pink fabric paint

Metallic white fabric paint

Small paintbrush

White thread

Black thread

6" x 7" (15 x 17.5) template

INSTRUCTIONS

1. Prepare your quilt by making a sandwich of the top white cotton fabric, the quilt batting, and the bottom white fabric.

2. Using white and black thread, stitch random straight stitches on the quilt top, ⅛"–½" (.3–1.25cm) apart. Fill the entire white fabric quilt top with horizontal and vertical lines. (A)

3. Pour a small amount of pink fabric paint into a different container, and add a small amount of water to thin the pigment, noting that thicker paint is best.

4. Turn the quilt over and paint the watered-down pink paint on the back of the quilt. The paint will seep through the holes and the thread of the stitched lines onto the front side of the quilt. If, after a few minutes, the paint does not soak through sufficiently, add a little more water to the paint, and then reapply on the

back. Wait another few minutes to see whether the paint seeps through. Repeat as needed, and then let dry completely. (B)

5. On the front side of the quilt, use a paintbrush to paint metallic white fabric paint, highlighting random stripes or sections. After the paint dries, you will be able to see the stitch and line texture, and some of the pink paint below the white metallic paint. (C)

6. Place the 6" x 7" (15 x 17.5cm) template on the quilt top to find the desired angle and placement of design.

7. To cut the quilt to size and finish the edges, refer to the "Finishing the Quilts" instructions in the "Getting Started" section on page 19. Use black thread when sewing straight and zigzag stitches.

A

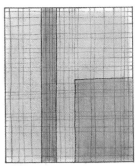

B   C

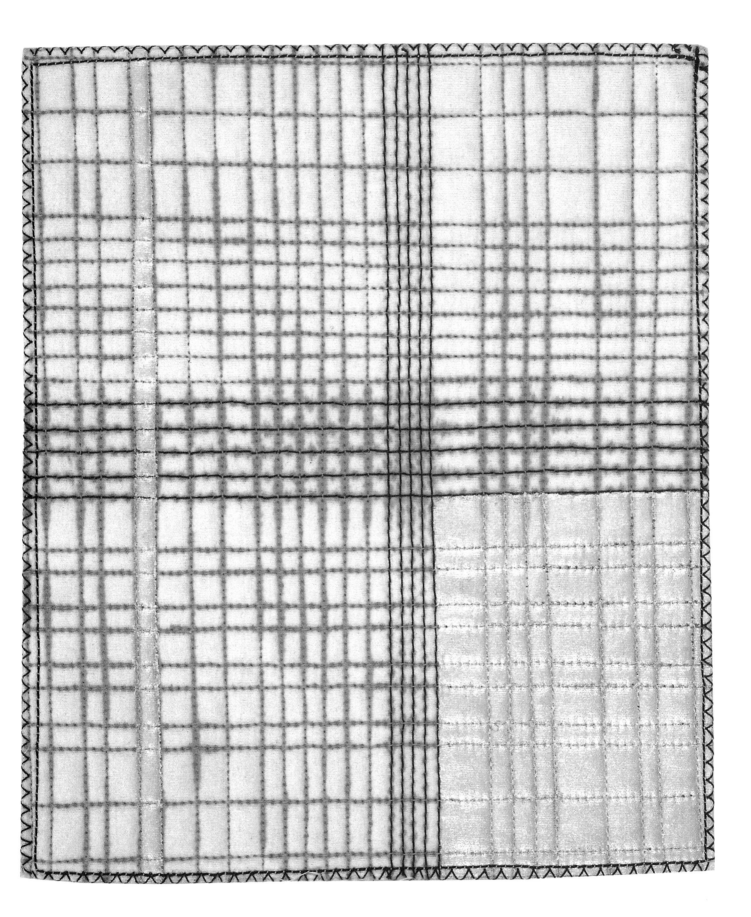

June 2001, 4" x 6" (10 x 15cm)

This quilt reflects a neighbor's unusual clematis flower, which was majestic and completely unique. It was created using stitches and fabric paint.

Clematis

MATERIALS

White cotton fabric
(two 8" x 10" [20.3 x 25.4cm] pieces)

Quilt batting
(one 8" x 10" [20.3 x 25.4cm] piece)

Opaque red fabric paint

Opaque green fabric paint

Small paintbrush

Red thread

Maroon thread

Green thread

Black thread

4" x 6" (10 x 15cm) template

INSTRUCTIONS

1. Prepare your quilt by making a sandwich of the top white cotton fabric, the quilt batting, and the bottom white fabric.

2. Starting at the center of the quilt top, sew straight red stitches to create the six flower petals. From the quilt center, sew slightly curved "petals" toward the outer edges of the quilt. After sewing one half of the petal 2¼"–2¾" (5.6–6.8cm)-long toward the edges of the quilt, pivot the needle and return to your starting point. Sew straight stitches through the center of the completed petal. Rotate the quilt top and repeat five more times to sew a total of six petals.

3. Paint a soft red line of opaque fabric paint down the middle of each petal. Once fully dried, stamp red dots using opaque fabric paint and the paintbrush end. Allow to dry.

4. In each corner of the quilt, stitch green straight stitches randomly to create the leaves. Sew straight stitches through the center of the leaves. Paint the leaves with opaque green fabric paint. Allow to dry. (A)

5. To finish the flower, stitch the stamens in the center using maroon thread. Sewing straight stitches, start at the center of the flower, and then stitch out ½"–¾" (1.2–1.8cm) toward the edges of the quilt. Use the reverse button on your sewing machine to sew back-ward and retrace the line of stitches you have just sewn. Pivot the needle position each time it returns to the center to create the illusion of a circle. (B)

6. Place the 4" x 6" (10 x 15cm) template on the quilt top to find the desired angle and placement of design.

7. To cut the quilt to size and finish the edges, refer to the "Finishing the Quilts" instructions in the "Getting Started" section on page 19. Use black thread when sewing straight and white thread for the zigzag stitches.

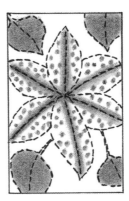

A

B

October 2004, 6" x 7" (15 x 17.5cm)

I was inspired by the peak autumn color in my neighborhood, especially by one tree with deep red leaves. For this quilt, I created continuous lines of leaves that mimic the rhythm of seasonal change and the steady, silent falling of foliage.

Red Leaves

MATERIALS

White cotton fabric (two 10" x 11" [25 x 27.5cm] pieces)

Quilt batting (one 10" x 11" [25 x 27.5cm] piece)

Dark red fabric paint

Small paintbrush

Dark red thread

Brown thread

Black thread

6" x 7" (15 x 17.5cm) template

INSTRUCTIONS

1. Prepare your quilt by making a sandwich of the top white cotton fabric, the quilt batting, and the bottom white fabric.

2. Starting at the upper left corner of the top white quilt fabric, stitch dark red lines on your sewing machine, creating continuous lines of leaves that are 2" (5cm) long and 1" (2.5cm) wide. The leaves should create a diagonal row about 11" (27.5cm) long. Repeat this step eight times, changing your starting position by 1 1/4" (3.1cm) to the left or right of the first row of sewn leaves.

3. Stitch through the center of each row of leaves, and then paint inside the lines using dark red fabric paint. (Refer to the "Sew First, Paint Next" section on page 81.) In a few random locations, paint only the inside edges of a few leaves. Allow to dry. **(A)**

4. To add the illusion of branches swaying on trees, stitch some brown wavy horizontal lines; randomly position the lines so they extend from the right and left sides of the quilt. **(B)**

5. Place the 6" x 7" (15 x 17.5cm) template on the quilt top to find the desired angle and placement of design.

6. To cut the quilt to size and finish the edges, refer to the "Finishing the Quilts" instructions in the "Getting Started" section on page 19. Use black thread when sewing straight and zigzag stitches.

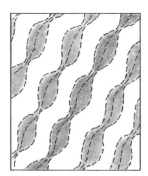

A

B

Memories often flood upon us in waves or in layers. After visiting my father's grave and making a crayon rubbing of his gravestone, I paid homage to him using quilted fabric, printed photos of the gravestone, and stones I brought from home.

Cemetery Visit

MATERIALS

White cotton fabric
(at least 5 [5m] yards)

White cotton fabric
(one 10" x 11" [25 x 27.5cm] piece)

Quilt batting
(one 10" x 11" [25 x 27.5cm] piece)

Large black crayon

Iron and ironing board
(or a towel and a flat surface)

Gravestones (Check with local authorities before approaching property for this project.)

A friend

White thread

Optional: camera for documenting site (photos can be printed and used as part of the quilt design)

Paper towels

6" x 7" (15 x 17.5cm) template

INSTRUCTIONS

1. Refer to the "Crayon Rubbings" section on page 79. Cut five pieces of fabric at least one yard (91.4cm) wide or larger. (If you know in advance the size of the gravestone you will visit, cut your fabric to the correct size.) Bring pre-cut pieces of fabric, a large black crayon, and a friend to the cemetery.

2. Select the area on the gravestone that you want to "copy." Ask your helper to hold the large piece of fabric on or around the front of the gravestone, pulling it as tightly as possible. (If you prefer to work on the project alone, try using a bungee cord or piece of rope.)

3. Using the long end of a large wide crayon, rub the crayon gently across the fabric, taking care to capture the texture of the gravestone on the fabric. Rub lightly at first, trying not to snag the fabric. Press harder as you rub, trying to pick up the texture. Stop when you like the results. **(A)**
Optional: Take photos of the gravesite, the gravestone, your helper, or anything else you might want to document. If you want to add photos to the quilt, print them out on a color printer using standard copy paper or photo paper. Cut out the desired images from the photos. Decide where you want to place them, and then use white stitches to attach them to the quilt.

4. At home, place the fabric with the crayon rubbing on an ironing board.

5. Cover the fabric with paper towels. With the heat setting adjusted to the proper temperature for your fabric and the steam setting off, iron until the crayon has melted into the fabric. (This should take less than a minute.)

6. Cut the rubbed fabric to 10" x 11" (25 x 27.5cm). When measuring and cutting, be sure to include sections of the rubbing that you want to highlight in the quilt.

7. Prepare your quilt by making a sandwich of the top rubbing fabric, the quilt batting, and the bottom white fabric.

8. Sew white stitches inside the centers of the letters or designs of the rubbing. Alternatively, you can also sew stitches around the letters or the designs. **(B)**

9. Place the 6" x 7" (15 x 17.5cm) template on the quilt top to find the desired angle and placement of design.

10. To cut the quilt to size and finish the edges, refer to the "Finishing the Quilts" instructions in the "Getting Started" section on page 19. Use black thread when sewing straight and zigzag stitches.

A

B

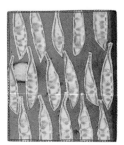

August 2004, 6" x 7" (15 x 17.5cm)

The brilliant color of my dryer lint, after washing a new green towel, reminded me of the fresh color and promise of seedpods on a neighbor's tree. Try playing with synthetic textures and natural products on your next quilt.

Seedpods & Lint

MATERIALS

White cotton fabric
(two 10" x 11" [25 x 27.5cm] pieces)

Quilt batting
(one 10" x 11" [25 x 27.5cm] piece)

Large green crayon

Seedpods from a tree
(or snow pea)

Paper towel

One sheet of dryer lint

One 8" x 9" (20 x 22cm) piece
of fabric netting

White thread

Black thread

6" x 7" (15 x 17.5cm) template

A

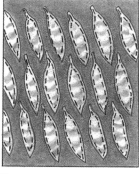

B

INSTRUCTIONS

1. Place one seedpod or snow pea under a 10" x 11" (25 x 27.5cm) piece of white fabric (this will later become the quilt top).

2. Using the long end of a large, wide crayon, rub gently across the fabric, taking care to capture the texture of the seedpod on the fabric. Rub lightly at first, trying not snag the fabric. Press harder as you rub, trying to pick up the texture. Stop when you like the results. (Refer to the "Crayon Rubbings" section on page 85 for more information.)

3. Move the seedpod to other sections of the fabric, then repeat. (A)

4. Place the fabric with the crayon rubbing on an ironing board.

5. Cover the fabric with a paper towel. With the heat setting adjusted to the proper temperature for your fabric and the steam setting off, iron until the crayon has melted into the fabric. (This should take less than one minute.)

6. Cut the seedpod rubbings out of the white fabric. If some of the seedpod rubbings too close together, cut them out in groups.

7. Prepare your quilt by making a sandwich of the dryer lint, the quilt batting, and the bottom white fabric.

8. Lay a 8" x 9" (20 x 22.5cm) piece of fabric netting on top of the lint sandwich.

9. Arrange the rubbings of seedpods on top of the netting and the dryer lint sandwich. Place the rubbings in three horizontal rows, with five or six seedpods per row. Alternate the orientation of the seedpods in each row. Pin in place if desired. Using white thread and straight stitches, sew around the seedpod rubbings, as close as possible to the cut edges. If you don't like the raw edges of the seedpods, zigzag white stitches over the edges. (B)

10. Place the 6" x 7" (15 x 17.5cm) template on the quilt top to find the desired angle and placement of design.

11. To cut the quilt to size and finish the edges, refer to the "Finishing the Quilts" instructions in the "Getting Started" section on page 19. Use black thread when sewing straight and zigzag stitches.

Antique lace often has an unbearably delicate quality—as if it weren't supposed to be touched. To highlight its beauty, I used a crayon rubbing technique to emphasize its intricate design.

Lace Design

MATERIALS

White cotton fabric
(two 10" x 12" [25 x 30cm] pieces)

Quilt batting
(one 10" x 12" [25 x 30cm] piece)

Large black crayon

One 7" x 2¼" (17.5 x 5.6cm)
piece of old lace

Paper towel

Metallic pink fabric paint

Metallic light pink fabric paint

Small paint brush

White thread

Black thread

6" x 8" (15 x 20cm) template

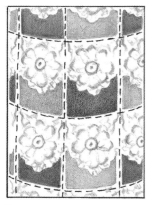

B

INSTRUCTIONS

1. Place the top edge of the lace horizontally under the middle of one 10" x 11" (25 x 27.5cm) piece of white fabric (this will later become the quilt top).

2. Using the long end of a large wide crayon, rub gently across the fabric, taking care to capture the texture of the lace onto the fabric. Rub lightly at first, trying not to snag the fabric. Press harder as you rub, trying to pick up the texture. Stop when you like the results. (Refer to the "Crayon Rubbings" section on page 85 for more information.) **(A)**

3. Keeping the lace under the fabric, shift the lace toward the bottom edge of the fabric so the top edge of the lace is about 2" (5cm) below the top edge of the first lace rubbing. Create another crayon rubbing of the lace.

4. Keeping the lace under the fabric, move the lace toward the top edge of the fabric so the bottom edge of the lace is about 2½" (6.2cm) above the top edge of the first lace rubbing. (There will be 2½" (6.2cm) of white space between the top and middle rubbing, leaving a row open for the actual piece of lace to be applied later.) Create another crayon rubbing of the lace.

5. Place fabric with the crayon rubbing on an ironing board. Cover the fabric with a paper towel. With the heat setting adjusted to the proper temperature for your fabric and the steam setting off, iron until the crayon has melted into the fabric. (This should take less than one minute.)

6. Prepare your quilt by making a sandwich of the top lace-rubbing cotton fabric, the quilt batting, and the bottom white fabric.

7. Place the piece of lace on the quilt top, over the 2½" (6.2cm) of white space between the top and middle rubbing. Pin in place if desired. Sew the lace in place, stitching close to the top edge of the lace.

8. Following the outline of the lace crayon rubbing, sew white stitches as close as possible to the rubbing, following the grid of the lace.

9. Referring to the "Sew first, Paint Next" section on page 81, alternate between light pink and pink fabric paint. Paint inside the stitched grid, filling up the empty spaces that do not display the lace crayon rubbing. Allow to dry. **(B)**

10. Place the 6" x 8" (15 x 20cm) template on the quilt top to find the desired angle and placement of design.

11. To cut the quilt to size and finish the edges, refer to the "Finishing the Quilts" instructions in the "Getting Started" section on page 19. Use black thread when sewing straight and zigzag stitches.

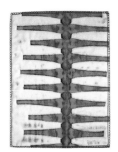

July 2005, 6" x 8" (15 x 20cm)

Fences don't always have to be barriers. This quilt is like a meta-fence, in which the ribs of a piece of orange construction fence are transmuted from their quotidian duty into a piece of art.

Ribs or Fence?

MATERIALS

White cotton fabric
(two 10" x 12" [25 x 30cm] pieces)

Quilt batting
(one 10" x 12" [25 x 30cm] piece)

Large black crayon

One 6" x 9½" (15 x 23.7cm) piece of orange construction fence

Orange fabric paint

Small paintbrush

White thread

Black thread

6" x 8" (15 x 20cm) template

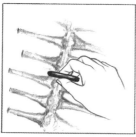

A

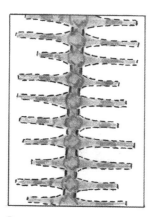

B

INSTRUCTIONS

1. Place the top edge of the piece of orange construction fence vertically under the middle of one 10" x 12" (25 x 30cm) piece of white fabric (this will later become the quilt top).

2. Using the long end of a large, wide crayon, rub gently across the fabric, taking care to capture the texture of the construction fence onto the fabric. Rub lightly at first, trying not to snag the fabric. Press harder as you rub, trying to pick up the texture. Stop when you like the results. (Refer to the "Crayon Rubbings" section on page 85 for more information.) (A)

3. Place fabric with the crayon rubbing on an ironing board. Cover the fabric with a paper towel. With the heat setting adjusted to the proper temperature for your fabric and the steam setting off, iron until the crayon has melted into the fabric. (This should take less than one minute.)

4. Prepare your quilt by making a sandwich of the top construction fence-rubbing cotton fabric, the quilt batting, and the bottom white fabric.

5. Using white thread, sew straight stitches touching the edge of the fence rubbing.

6. Paint over the crayon rubbing and inside the lines of the stitched construction fence using orange fabric paint. (Refer to the "Sew First, Then Paint" section on page 89.) Allow to dry. (B)

7. Place the 6" x 8" (15 x 20cm) template on the quilt top to find the desired angle and placement of design. The vertical section of the construction fence should be positioned slightly to the right of the quilt center.

8. To cut the quilt to size and finish the edges, refer to the "Finishing the Quilts" instructions in the "Getting Started" section on page 19. Use black thread when sewing straight and zigzag stitches.

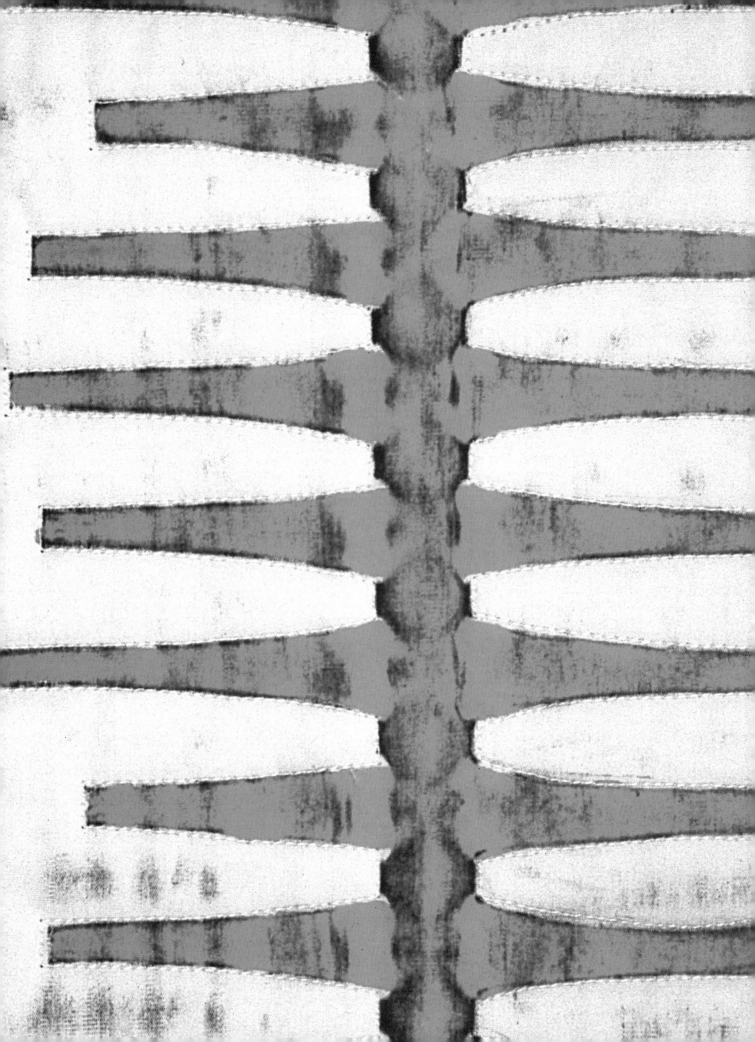

July 1999, 8" x 10" (20 x 25cm)

There is little that is more pure than the ocean and the sky in Martha's Vineyard, Massachusets. Using a simple fabric painting technique combined with stitching, I captured this oasis in my quilt.

Ocean Waves

MATERIALS

White cotton fabric
(two 12" x 14" [30 x 35cm] pieces)

Quilt batting (one 12" x 14"
[30 x 35cm] piece)

Four (or more) different shades of blue fabric paint (regular, metallic, or opaque)

Small paintbrush

White thread

8" x 10" (20 x 25cm) template

INSTRUCTIONS

1. Prepare your quilt by making a sandwich of the top white cotton fabric, the quilt batting, and the bottom white fabric.

2. Starting near the center of the quilt top, sew rows of straight white stitches horizontally across the white fabric.

3. Between each of the stitched straight lines, sew wavelike lines across the quilt. The highest part of the wave should be 1" (2.5cm) to $1\frac{1}{4}$" (3.1cm) high, and the lowest part of the wave between $\frac{3}{8}$" (.9cm) and $\frac{3}{4}$" (1.8cm). **(A)**

4. Refer to the "Sew First, Then Paint" section on page 89.) Alternating between four (or more) different colors of blue fabric paint, paint inside the lines of the stitched waves, trying not to paint on the lines themselves. Allow to dry. **(B)**

5. Place the 8" x 10" (20 x 25cm) template on the quilt top to find the desired angle and placement of design.

6. To cut the quilt to size and finish the edges, refer to the "Finishing the Quilts" instructions in the "Getting Started" section on page 19. Instead of making a binding for this quilt, use white thread when sewing straight and zigzag stitches.

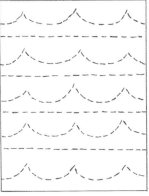

A

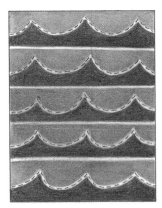

B

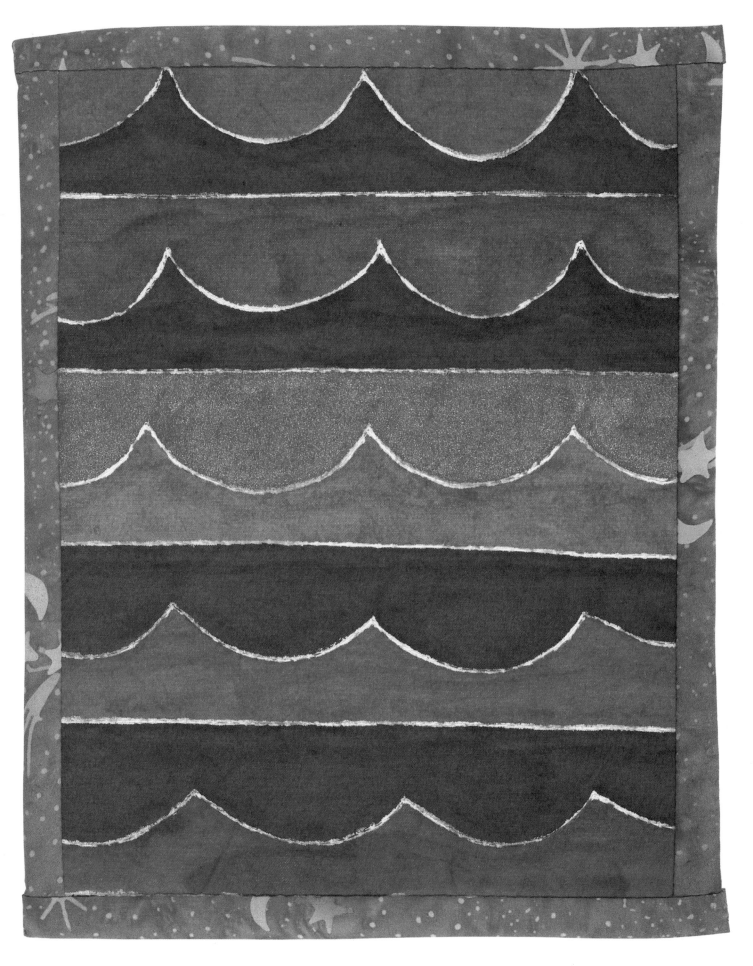

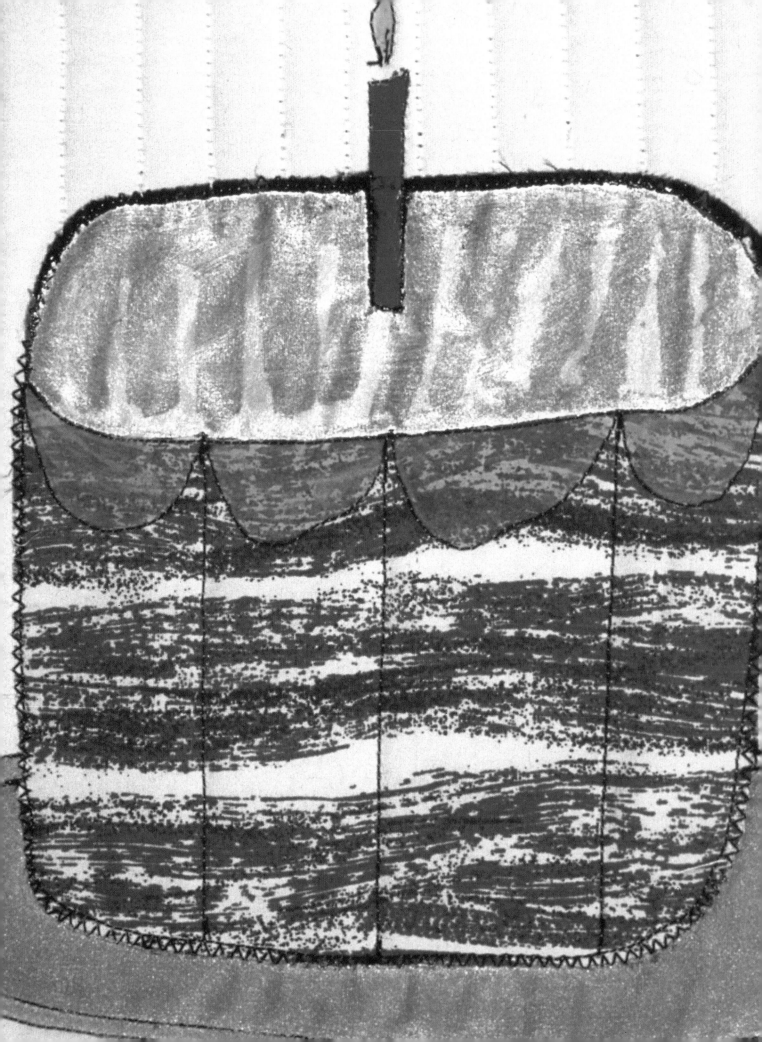

December 2004, 6" x 7" (15 x 17.5cm)

The opulent paints in this decadent quilt make it look good enough to eat! I layered deep colors, much the way I'd assemble a birthday cake, to create this striking resemblance to the cake I baked for my son's birthday.

Let Them Have (Chocolate) Cake

MATERIALS

White cotton fabric
(two 10" x 11" [25 x 27.5cm] pieces)

Quilt batting
(one 10" x 11" [25 x 27.5cm] piece)

One 5" (12.5cm) square of brown and white printed fabric

Metallic white fabric paint

Light brown fabric paint

Metallic gold fabric paint

Metallic silver fabric paint

Opaque blue fabric paint

Opaque yellow fabric paint

Small paintbrush

White, brown, and black thread

6" x 7" (15 x 17.5cm) template

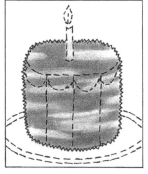

A

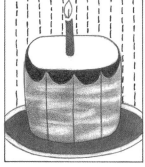

B

INSTRUCTIONS

1. Prepare your quilt by making a sandwich of the top white cotton fabric, the quilt batting, and the bottom white fabric.

2. Cut a "cake" shape out of one 5" square (12.7cm) of brown-and-white printed fabric. Position on the white quilt top, sewing zigzag brown stitches around the edges. Stitch the top of the cake by sewing brown stitches in a large oval. Follow the top edge of the "cake fabric" and continue the bottom edge of the oval $1^1/_2$" (3.7cm) below the top edge.

3. Stitch the candle by sewing a $^1/_4$" x $1^1/_2$" (.6 x 3.7cm) vertical rectangle at the center top part of the cake top.

4. Stitch the flame of the candle, starting $^1/_8$" (.3cm) from the candle top, and sewing a curved line $^1/_2$" (1.2cm) toward the top of the quilt. Once you've reached the highest point of the flame, pivot the needle and return so you are stitching to the beginning of the flame.

5. Stitch the icing by sewing straight stitches, starting from one of the side bottom edges of the cake top toward the other side edge. Sew four scallop shapes $^1/_2$"–$^3/_4$" (1.2–1.8cm) deep, and $1^1/_4$" (3.1cm) wide. Sew three vertical lines from the scalloped icing lines down to the bottom of the cake.

6. Stitch the plate, using black thread straight stitches, starting on one cake side about 1"–$1^1/_2$" (2.5 x 3.7cm) from the bottom edge, and sewing a large oval $^3/_4$" (1.8cm) below the bottom edge and then back around the other bottom edge. To create the rim, sew another row of stitches $^1/_8$" (.3cm) parallel.

7. Paint inside the stitched lines of the cake top, using metallic white fabric paint. (Allow to dry.) Paint inside the stitched lines of the candle using opaque blue fabric paint. Paint inside of the flame using yellow fabric paint. Paint inside the scalloped icing using light brown fabric paint. Paint inside the main part of the plate using metallic silver fabric paint. (Allow to dry.) Paint inside the rim of the plate using metallic gold fabric paint. (Allow to dry.) **(A)**

8. Use white thread to stitch vertical lines for the background behind the cake. Measure $^1/_2$" (1.25cm) in either direction from the flame, repeating until you have six columns of white stitches on both sides of the candle. **(B)**

9. Place the 6" x 7" (15 x 17.5cm) template on the quilt top to find the desired angle and placement of design.

10. To cut the quilt to size and finish the edges, refer to the "Finishing the Quilts" instructions in the "Getting Started" section on page 19. Use black thread when sewing straight and zigzag stitches.

Fiber

Sewing with fiber usually implies sewing with fabric, but in this book fiber includes almost any material that can be sewn and that will not break, crumble, or rot. Some of my favorites fibers include yarn, ribbon, and thread, but you can use anything, including old socks, towels, or yard-sale linens.

When choosing materials made of fiber, keep your eyes open for everyday items you would not usually consider using in a quilt, such as felt and dryer lint.

There's really no limit to fiber choices, with one important exception. While you might want to get fiber with your breakfast cereal, you never want to get breakfast cereal with your quilt! Fiber is, of course, found in many food items that should be categorically avoided in quiltmaking. Leaves and flowers will dry out over time, with the exception of oak leaves, which hold up under stitching. (Use an oak leaf that has freshly fallen from a tree).

Experimenting with Fiber

Fibers that are fun to experiment with, safe for sewing, and easy to find come in a variety of forms.

FABRIC is a staple for quilters, and its sources are numerous. These include new printed material, recycled fabric (from old clothing, scraps, or partial bolts found at yard sales), or donations from friends and family. Fabric can even be found in packaging for gourmet foods and drinks.

Recycled or previously sewn fabric is a great source of quilting ideas. Consider using old linens and curtains, especially if they offer a nice design or color palette. Another source of fabric is used clothing: by deconstructing your clothes (taking them apart at the seams) you can increase your supply of fabric without spending any money. If you have an old T-shirt, never-to-be-worn-again brides-maid dress, or out-of-style pants, use a seam ripper to salvage the fabric or simply cut them up.

Silk flowers are easy to take apart and attach to your quilt.

The back side of clothing labels offers interesting patterns, textures, and colors.

Opposite Page: "Leaves and Batting," 2000, 8" x 7"

Consider all your options for collecting fabric. Clean socks with holes don't need to go in the trash: Instead cut pieces from them for later use. Do the labels in your clothes scratch your neck? Removing them will solve the problem, and if they are woven, the underside may contain interesting patterns.

Sheer fabrics, whether cut from clothing or curtains or purchased by the yard, can be layered on top of any quilted design to create a see-through effect. Or consider using a piece of a sheer fabric over a portion of your quilt design, which preserves the design but mutes its presence.

THREAD is a must-have in sewing and quilting. Collect as many colors as you have room to store. When you sew a quilt, you can create a totally different effect by using white or black thread or by selecting a matching or contrasting color. If you have time to experiment with scraps before sewing the quilt, try sewing the same design with a different color of thread and notice the change in the aesthetic of each sample.

You can even save your trimmed thread ends, as they can be lovely used on their own. If you are stuck for an idea, try placing a handful of cut thread under a piece of sheer fabric, and then stitch the two together.

YARN If you knit, or know someone who does, collect scraps of yarn, especially textured or fashion yarn. You can use these pieces to outline a design: Hold them in place by sewing a zigzag stitch over them (also known as *couching*). You can also place a piece of sheer fabric over a strand of yarn or mix up scraps of colored yarn and layer sheer fabric over them for a varied and colorful effect.

RIBBON is abundant during holidays, around birthdays, and at weddings, graduations, Mother's Day, and other celebrations. Save your favorite colors and textures for future projects.

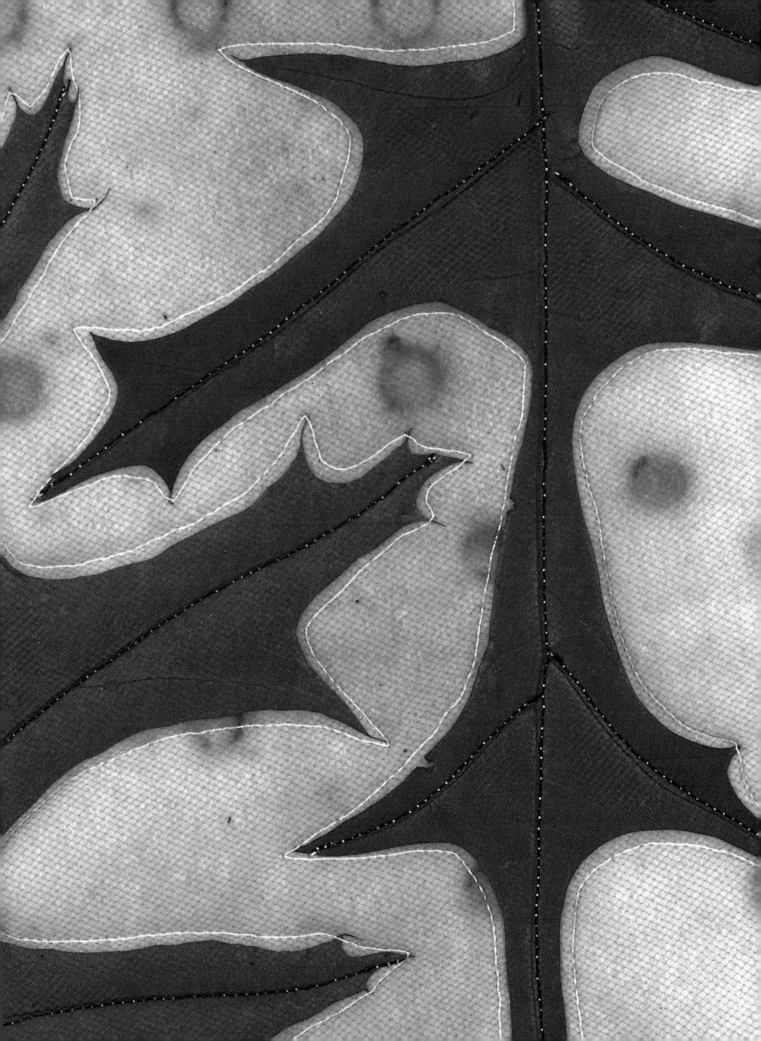

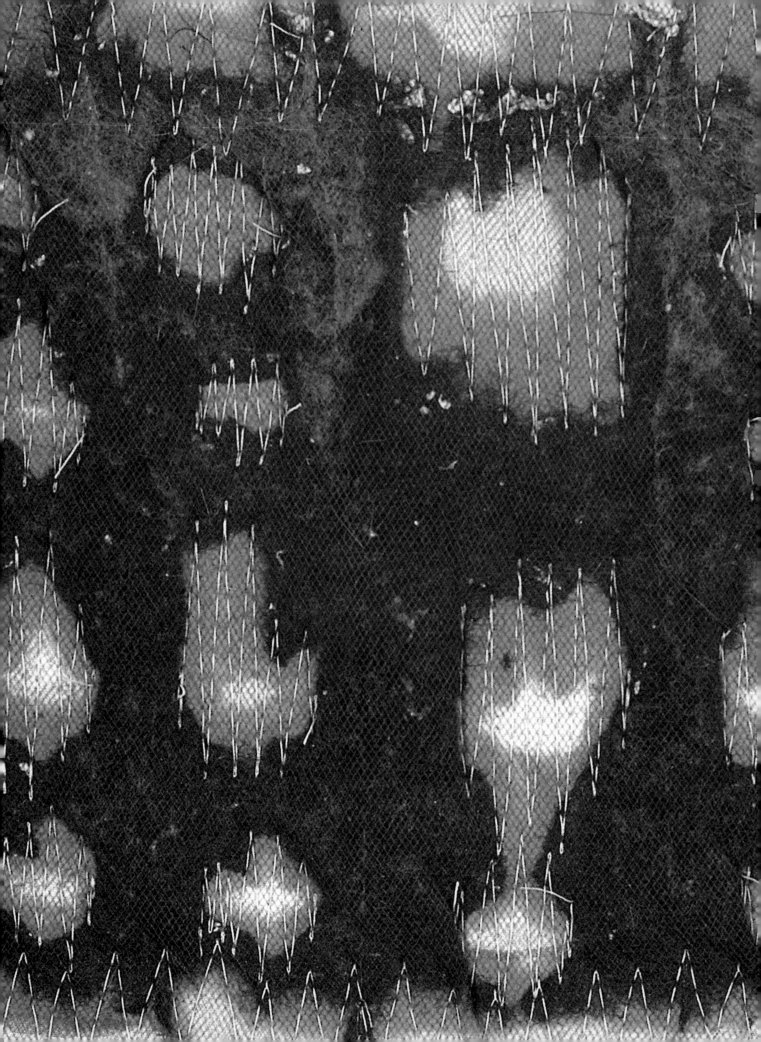

Previous page: "Dryer Lint Sandwich," 2000, 8" x 7"

Unusual Fibers

Many of the following are everyday household items that can be used in creative ways. Once you start looking around your home, you will find an endless supply of fiber-based materials!

Felt weather-stripping is not a typical material employede in a sewing project, but when mine fell off the doorframe one spring day, I took notice of its unusual composition and texture. It is made from what appear to be scraps of felt, and although it's typically brown or gray, flecks of red, blue, or yellow are also visable. To sew its thick texture, you will need a strong sewing machine needle. If you don't have weather-stripping, substitute heavy felt or felt scraps from craft projects. Experiment with one solid color or use different colored pieces of felt to create the collage effect of weather-stripping.

While changing your ironing board cover, have you ever noticed the padding underneath? This batting is made of foam or cotton-like fiber. If yours is made with a fiber batting, check it for accumulated rust and texture; its "natural" patina makes a wonderful quilt background.

Weather stripping, which often lines the windows and doors in colder-climate homes, features several layers and colors of felt-like material.

The color of your dryer lint can be quite beautiful after washing certain towels, sheets, and fabrics.

The color and texture of silk flowers add interest to your quilts with minimal cost.

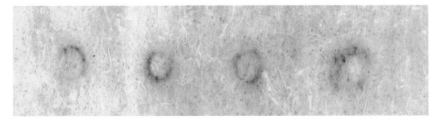

Rust stains on an ironing board pad create an interesting natural pattern.

If you don't have a rusty ironing board, you can substitute cotton quilt batting, and create your own version of rusty circles with fabric paint and an empty paper towel roll or thread spool. Hold the tube by one end, gently dip it in orange (or other color) fabric paint—just enough to coat—and stamp as many circles as desired on the batting. Be sure to let the batting dry completely before using.

Everybody knows it's important to remove the lint from your dryer after a few loads of laundry, but most people don't think of using the lint in a quilting project! Rather than throw it away, take a closer look at the density, color, and texture—and save a few of the best pieces for quilting. The lint formed after drying new towels is especially "desirable"—it's dense, and offers undiluted color.

To store dryer lint, sandwich it between layers of waxed paper. When you sew with dryer lint, place a piece of thin netting on top to stabilize it; otherwise, it will come apart easily.

If you don't have any dryer lint, substitute scraps of felt (try solid colors or combine different colored pieces). Because felt won't fall apart like dryer lint, there's no need to sew the thin layer of netting on top unless you like the effect.

To create more interesting shapes and colors with fibers, I often take apart silk flowers (cut the blossom off their stems to open them). Silk flowers contain various colors and shapes, all of which are easy to sew.

Tree bark is something most people would never think of using for quilting material, and with good reason—it's usually thick and difficult to find on the ground. Birch bark, however, is a notable exception. If you see this bark peeling from a tree, take a piece and try sewing with it. You might need to place a piece of thin netting over it for stabilization. You can also substitute synthetic birch bark or paint fabric, both of which resemble birch bark.

If you have a digital photograph, you can print it on fabric using a color printer. To do this, purchase a package of T-shirt transfer paper, and follow the directions. Remember to reverse the photo before printing it on transfer paper; otherwise, it will be backward after you iron it on your fabric. Depending on the image you choose, this may not matter—but for some images it's essential. Many people like to print fabric photos of their loved ones for memory quilts, but I challenge you to take pictures of natural objects, (flowers, bark, leaves), architectural elements (dental moldings, chair rails, bricks), or other items around your house with interesting designs or textures (couch fabric, rugs, paintings).

August 1999, 8" x 10" (20 x 25cm)

Pay homage to your sewing machine (or collection of colorful threads), and create a quilt using remnants from your other projects.

Checks with Stitching

MATERIALS

White or off-white cotton fabric (two 12" x 14" [30 x 35cm] pieces)

Quilt batting (one 12" x 14" [30 x 35cm] piece)

One 9" x 3½" (22.5 x 8.7cm) piece of black and white checked fabric

White thread

Black thread

Pink thread

Orange thread

Green thread

Blue thread

Red thread

Purple thread

Yellow thread

8" x 10" (20 x 25cm) template

INSTRUCTIONS

1. Prepare your quilt by making a sandwich of top white or off-white cotton fabric, the quilt batting, and the bottom white or off-white fabric.

2. Place one 9" x 3½" (22.5 x 8.7cm) piece of black-and-white checked fabric horizontally at the top edge of the quilt. Stitch straight lines horizontally across the black-and-white checked section, from one side to the other, alternating the thread colors. **(A)**

3. Starting at the top of the quilt, stitch lines down into the white area. Alternate the thread colors and the length of the stitched lines, making sure to leave the threads at the top long, so they hang down from the top of the quilt. **(B)**

4. Place the 8" x 10" (20 x 25cm) template on the quilt top to find the desired angle and placement of design.

5. To cut the quilt to size and finish the edges, refer to the "Finishing the Quilts" instructions in the "Getting Started" section on page 19. Instead of making a binding for this quilt, use black thread when sewing straight and zigzag stitches.

A

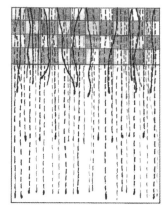

B

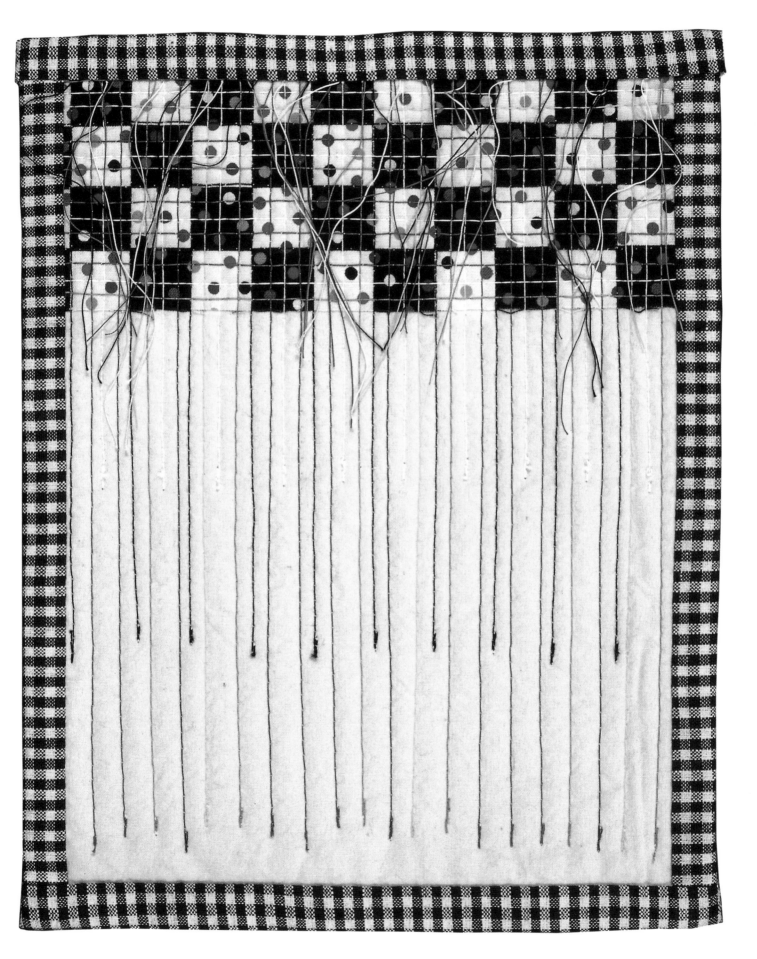

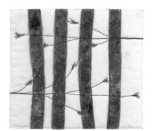

April 2000, 8" x 7" (20 x 17.5cm)

Sometimes manmade objects mimic nature without even trying. The weather-stripping from my front door looked so much like tree bark that I made it into a tree design.

Budding Branches

MATERIALS

White cotton fabric
(two 12" x 11" [30 x 27.5cm] pieces)

Quilt batting
(one 12" x 11" [30 x 27.5cm] piece)

Four 8½" (21.2cm) pieces of weather-stripping (or substitute four 8½" (21.2cm) pieces of brown craft felt)

Brown thread

Green thread

White thread

8" x 7" (20 x 17.5cm) template

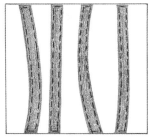

A

B

INSTRUCTIONS

1. Prepare your quilt by making a sandwich of the top white cotton fabric, the quilt batting, and the bottom white fabric.

2. Lay four lengths of weather-stripping or felt vertically on the quilt top, spacing them about 1" (2.5cm) apart. Don't be concerned if they are slightly warped vertically—it will add to the charm of the quilt. Using a heavy sewing machine needle and white thread, sew straight stitches along both edges of all four pieces, making sure to sew close to the edges. **(A)**

3. Stitch one tree branch with straight stitches and brown thread—starting near the quilt bottom on the left side—and stop before you get to the right side. Repeat three times, starting at the same location, but vary the angle of the line to create four ends from one main branch.

4. Stitch additional branches, starting near the quilt top on the right side and stopping before you get to the left side. Repeat four times, starting at the same location, so the branches on the right side are created with the same technique as the left side.

5. Using green thread, stitch the "buds." Starting at the end of one "branch," sew a few straight stitches outward, and then return back to the same spot (using the reverse button if using a sewing machine). Pivot the needle slightly before sewing the next part of the bud, and then repeat to sew random stitches three or more times. Repeat bud stitching seven more times so each branch has a "bud." **(B)**

6. Place the 8" x 7" (20 x 17.5cm) template on the quilt top to find the desired angle and placement of design.

7. To cut the quilt to size and finish the edges, refer to the "Finishing the Quilts" instructions in the "Getting Started" section on page 19. Use white thread when sewing straight and zigzag stitches.

May 2000, 8" x 7" (20 x 17.5cm)

This quilt uses a technique I learned in art school called "contour line drawing," in which you draw an outline of an object but do not take your pencil off the paper once you've started drawing. I made such a line drawing here, instead using my sewing machine as the "pencil."

Sewn Chair

MATERIALS

White cotton fabric
(two 12" x 11" [30 x 27.5cm] pieces)

Quilt batting
(one 12" x 11" [30 x 27.5cm] piece)

Dark brown thread

Light brown thread

White thread

8" x 7" (20 x 17.5cm) template

INSTRUCTIONS

1. Prepare your quilt by making a sandwich of the top white cotton fabric, the quilt batting, and the bottom white fabric.

2. Choose an object to create as an outline drawing, and take a deep breath. (If you feel really uncomfortable about trying this on the sewing machine, practice on a piece of paper.)

3. Choose one location on the quilt to start your "drawing." Look carefully at the object (chair shown), and sew very slowly, using very short straight stitches and brown thread. When you get to a place where you need to change directions, keep your sewing needle in the down position and pivot the fabric. If you need to move to a different section of your drawing, sew over an already sewn line or sew a line to the place you need to draw next. Try not to end a line and start a

new one. The fun in making a contour line drawing is seeing the inaccuracy of the object when you're finished. Don't pressure yourself to make a perfect drawing. **(A)**

4. After you have "drawn" the object to your liking, end the stitching. Then, to create a baseline and/or background for your object, stitch several horizontal lines using light brown thread. Start and stop the lines as desired. **(B)**

5. Place the 8" x 7" (20 x 17.5cm) template on the quilt top to find the desired angle and placement of design.

6. To cut the quilt to size and finish the edges, refer to the "Finishing the Quilts" instructions in the "Getting Started" section on page 19. Use white thread when sewing straight and zigzag stitches.

A

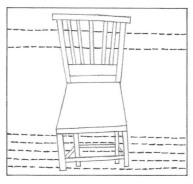

B

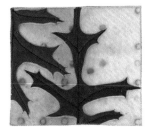

October 2000, 8" x 7" (20 x 17.5cm)

When I removed my ironing board cover, I noticed rusty dots on the batting. At the same time, oak leaves were blowing all over my yard; I felt inspired to combine the two rust-colored items in this quilt.

Leaves & Batting

MATERIALS

White cotton fabric
(two 12" x 11" [30 x 27.5cm] pieces)

Quilt batting
(one 12" x 11" [30 x 27.5cm] piece)

One 9" x 8" (22.5 x 20cm) piece of ironing board batting with rust stains (or substitute cotton quilt batting and small jar brown fabric paint)

Two freshly fallen brown oak leaves (or substitute artificial leaves)

One 9" x 8" (22.5 x 20cm) piece of thin light-colored fabric netting

White thread

Brown thread

8" x 7" (20 x 17.5cm) template

INSTRUCTIONS

1. Prepare your quilt by making a sandwich of the top white cotton fabric, the quilt batting, and the bottom white fabric.

2. Cut one 9" x 8" (22.5 x 20cm) piece of ironing board batting with rust stains (or substitute the 9" x 8" (22.5 x 20cm) piece of cotton quilt batting). Place the ironing board batting (or substitute quilt batting) on the center of the quilt sandwich.

3. Place two oak leaves on top of the batting, facing them in opposite directions vertically. Play with the placement of the leaves. **(A)**

4. Place the 9" x 8" (22.5 x 20cm) netting over the batting and leaves. Pin the netting in place.

Do not pin through the leaves. Stitch on top of the leaves, using a straight stitch and brown thread, following the veins.

5. Switch to white thread and stitch a straight stitch closely around the edges of the leaves to accent their shape. **(B)**

6. Place the 8" x 7" (20 x 17.5cm) template on the quilt top to find the desired angle and placement of design.

7. To cut the quilt to size and finish the edges, refer to the "Finishing the Quilts" instructions in the "Getting Started" section on page 19. Use white thread when sewing straight and zigzag stitches.

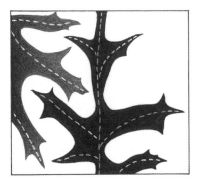

A

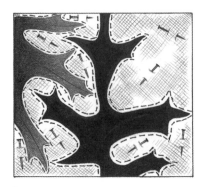

B

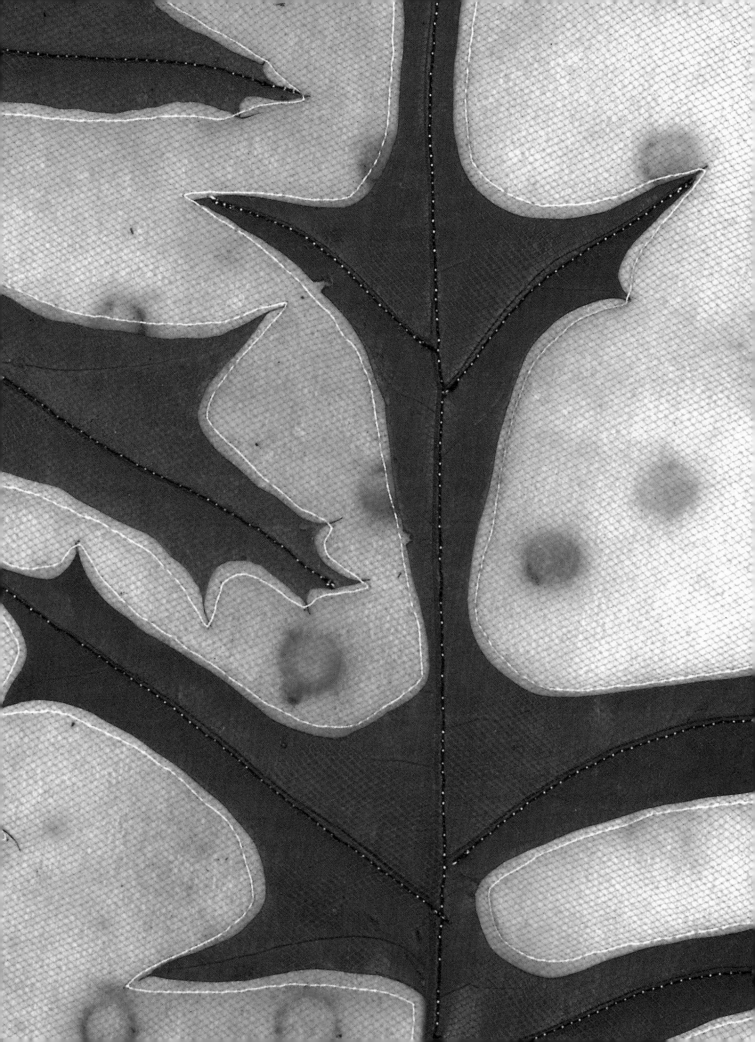

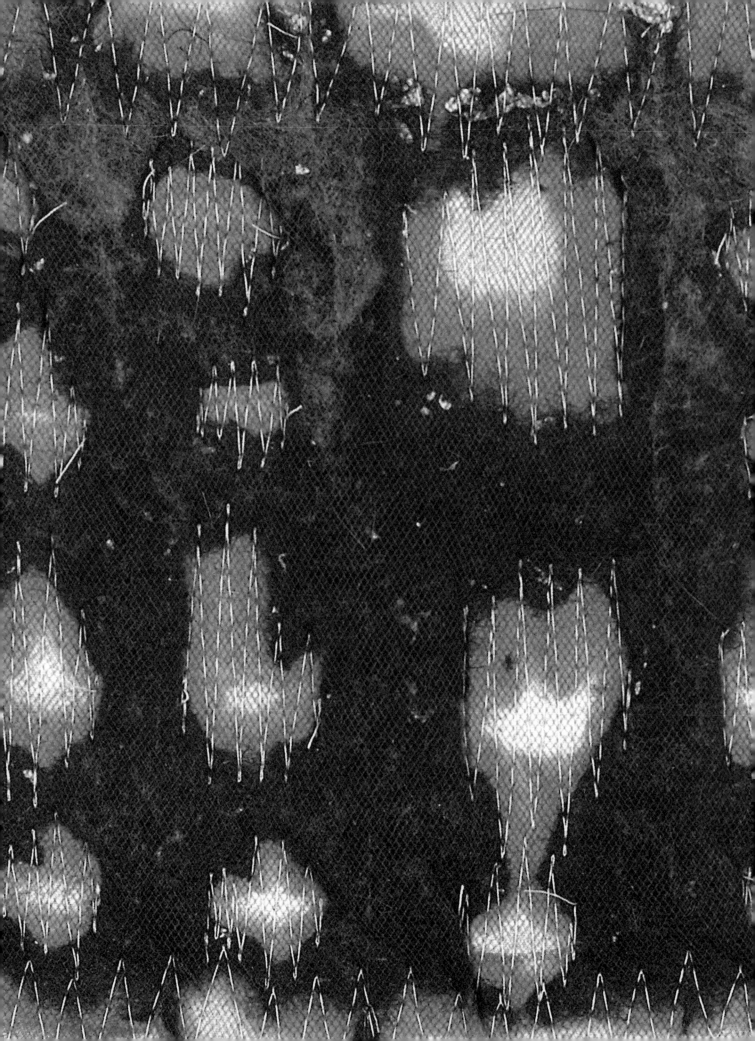

Good enough to eat! Well, not quite: This "dryer lint sandwich" has less to do with hunger pangs and more to do with the beautiful, felt-like quality of dryer lint, which is a malleable material for quilt making.

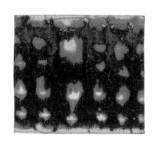

Dryer Lint Sandwich

MATERIALS

White cotton fabric
(two 12" x 11" [30 x 27.5cm] pieces)

Quilt batting
(one 12" x 11" [30 x 27.5cm] piece)

Three sheets of dryer lint, at least 9" x 8" (22.5 x 20cm), in three different colors (or substitute with pieces of craft felt)

One 9" x 8" (22.5 x 20cm) piece of fabric netting

White thread

8" x 7" (20 x 17.5cm) template

INSTRUCTIONS

1. Prepare your quilt by making a sandwich of the top white cotton fabric, the quilt batting, and the bottom white fabric.

2. Make a "lint sandwich" using three pieces of dryer lint at least 9" x 8" (22.5 x 20cm) or larger. Place the light color on the bottom, the bright color in the middle, and the darker color on the top.

3. Use your fingers to make small pinches of the "lint sandwich" and cut those parts of the pinched lint away to show the different layers. Discard the cut pieces of lint or save them for a different project. (A)

4. Carefully place the "lint sandwich" on the quilt top. Lay a 9" x 8" (22.5 x 20cm) piece of fabric netting on top of the lint sandwich.

5. Using white thread and straight stitches, sew back and forth over the net and cut-lint sections, using the reverse button on your sewing machine to help stitch backward. Sew until each cut section is sewn in place. Repeat for each of the cut sections. (B)

6. Place the 8" x 7" (20 x 17.5cm) template on the quilt top to find the desired angle and placement of design.

7. To cut the quilt to size and finish the edges, refer to the "Finishing the Quilts" instructions in the "Getting Started" section on page 19. Use white thread when sewing straight and zigzag stitches.

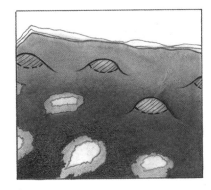

A

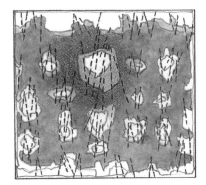

B

May 2001, 4" x 6" (10 x 15cm)

Spring was in full bloom, and it was a beautiful sight. The burst of color in a silk flower reminded me of the shocking beauty of spring.

Flat Flower Parts

MATERIALS

White cotton fabric
(two 8" x 10" [20 x 25cm] pieces)

Quilt batting (one 8" x 10" [20 x 25cm] piece)

One silk (or artificial) flower with leaves

White thread

Green thread

Black thread

4" x 6" (10 x 15cm) template

INSTRUCTIONS

1. Prepare your quilt by making a sandwich of the top white cotton fabric, the quilt batting, and the bottom white fabric.

2. Take apart the silk (or artificial) flower with leaves. To do this, carefully cut the flowers and leaves off the stem. The petals and leaves are easily separated once removed from the stem. Open and flatten the flower and leaf sections. Iron on a low heat setting if needed to remove creases or wrinkles.

3. Place the leaves on the center bottom of the top piece of white cotton fabric, and then stitch close to the edges using green straight stitches.

4. Stitch three extra leaf shapes with green thread, starting where the attached silk (or artificial) leaves join one another. **(A)**

5. Lay the flattened flower on the quilt, positioning it slightly over the top part of the sewn leaves. Stitch close to edges, using white thread. **(B)**

6. Place the 4" x 6" (10 x 15cm) template on the quilt top to find the desired angle and placement of design.

7. To cut the quilt to size and finish the edges, refer to the "Finishing the Quilts" instructions in the "Getting Started" section on page 19. Use black thread when sewing straight and white thread for the zigzag stitches.

A

B

August 2002, 6" x 4" (15 x 10cm)

I was drawn to the backs of these clothing labels because of the reversed writing and the layers of stitching. For this quilt I made a patchwork design out of the labels and edged it with an old paper measuring tape.

Patchwork Labels

MATERIALS

White cotton fabric
(two 10" x 8" [25 x 20cm] pieces)

Quilt batting
(one 10" x 8" [25 x 20cm] piece)

Nine woven clothing labels,
cut to about 1¾" (4.3cm) square

Four 6" (15cm) long pieces of paper or fabric measuring tape (or substitute ribbon)

White thread

Black thread

6" x 4" (15 x 10cm) template

INSTRUCTIONS

1. Prepare your quilt by making a sandwich of the top white cotton fabric, the quilt batting, and the bottom white fabric.

2. Iron nine woven clothing labels flat, using the appropriate heat setting.

3. Paying attention to the more interesting areas of the label, measure and then cut the nine clothing labels to about 1¾" (4.3cm) square. Discard the label scraps or save for another project.

4. Flip the nine labels upside down so the threads are visible from the back and the logos or writings aren't recognizable.

5. Starting at the center of the quilt top, arrange the labels in three rows of three, turned 90 degrees from the horizontal shape of the quilt. Stitch in place—close to the edges of the labels—with white thread. (A)

6. Place the measuring tape pieces ¼" (.6cm) from the four outer edges of the label design.

7. Stitch close to the edges of the measuring tape pieces, using white thread and straight stitches. (B)

8. Place the 6" x 4" (15 x 10cm) template on quilt top to find the desired angle and placement of design.

9. To cut the quilt to size and finish the edges, refer to the "Finishing the Quilts" instructions in the "Getting Started" section on page 19. Use black thread when sewing straight and white thread for the zigzag stitches.

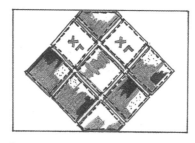

A

B

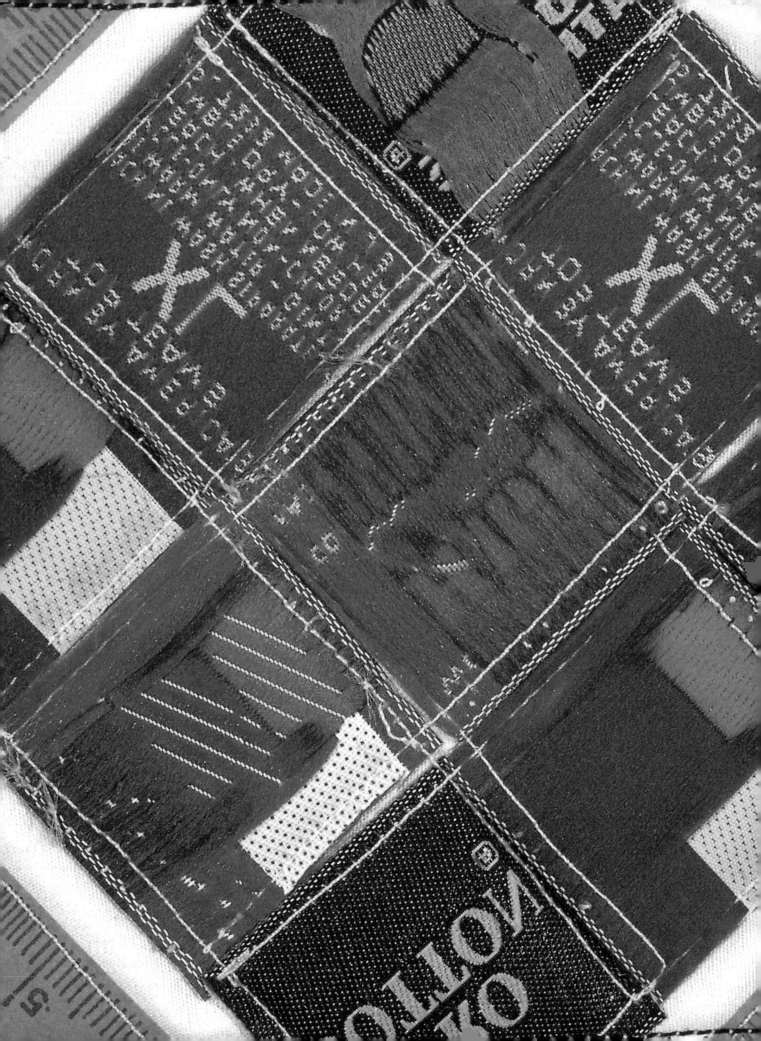

One day while walking in the woods
I was struck by how birch bark peels off the tree,
like layers of skin. I attached the fragile birch bark
to the quilt by holding it in place with sheer fabric.

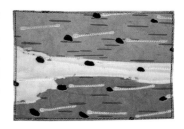

Skin-Like Bark

MATERIALS

White cotton fabric
(two 10" x 8" [25 x 20cm] pieces)

Quilt batting
(one 10" x 8" [25 x 20cm] piece)

Two 7" x 2½" (17.5 x 6.2cm) pieces
birch tree bark

One 8" x 6" (20 x 15cm) piece of
sheer fabric (sheer with black dots
and white lines shown)

White thread

Black thread

6" x 4" (15 x 10cm) template

INSTRUCTIONS

1. Prepare your quilt by making a sandwich of the top white cotton fabric, the quilt batting, and the bottom white fabric.

2. Find two 7" x 2½" (17.5 x 6.2 cm) pieces of birch tree bark. Removed the bark from the tree carefully so you don't damage the tree. *Note: Do not trespass or peel too much bark from one tree. If possible, use bark that has fallen to the ground or is already peeling from the trunk.*

3. Place the bark pieces horizontally on the top piece of white cotton fabric, at least ⅝" (1.5cm) apart. If the bark has different colors on both sides, use the lighter side for the piece on the top of the design and the darker side for the bottom piece. **(A)**

4. Place a piece of sheer fabric horizontally on top of the birch bark. Stitch through the sheer fabric—using white straight stitches—and sew around the bark, near the edges. If the sheer fabric has a pattern, stitch over the pattern with white thread. If the sheer fabric doesn't have a design, randomly sew more stitches over the bark. **(B)**

5. Place the 6" x 4" (15 x 10cm) template on the quilt top to find the desired angle and placement of design.

6. To cut the quilt to size and finish the edges, refer to the "Finishing the Quilts" instructions in the "Getting Started" section on page 19. Use black thread when sewing straight and white thread for the zigzag stitches.

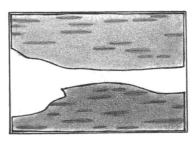

A

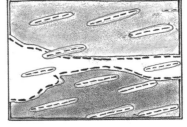

B

March 2003, 6" x 6" (15 x 15cm)

When sorting laundry one day, I found the difference between the inside and outside of my son's socks very interesting. To keep my son from wearing these worn and holey socks, I decided to use them for a quilt.

Stitched Socks

MATERIALS

White cotton fabric
(two 10" x 10" [25 x 25cm] pieces)

Quilt batting
(one 10" x 10" [25 x 25cm] piece)

One pair of socks with holes
(gray shown)

White thread

Black thread

6" x 6" (15 x 15cm) template

INSTRUCTIONS

1. Prepare your quilt by making a sandwich of the top white cotton fabric, the quilt batting, and the bottom white fabric.

2. Choose one pair of socks with holes. Look for worn toe sections with interesting shapes or socks with terry cloth on the inside.

3. Measure each sock, starting at the tip of the toe, and then cut it 3½" (8.7cm) long, keeping the toe section whole.

4. Place the two toe sections on the left center side of the quilt top, facing each section toe to toe. Pin in place.

5. Measure and cut the top 1½" (3.7cm) edge from one sock, and then cut the piece so it becomes a 1½" x 7½" (3.7 x 18.7cm) strip.

6. Place the 1½" x 7½" (3.7 x 18.7cm) sock strip vertically, about ½" (1.2cm) away from the right side of the toe sections. Pin in place. **(A)**

7. Stitch straight lines, using white thread, over the three sock sections. The lines should be sewn randomly from side to side and top to bottom, enough to attach the sock pieces to quilt. **(B)**

8. Place the 6" x 6" (15 x 15cm) template on the quilt top to find the desired angle and placement of design.

9. To cut the quilt to size and finish the edges, refer to the "Finishing the Quilts" instructions in the "Getting Started" section on page 19. Use black thread when sewing straight and zigzag stitches.

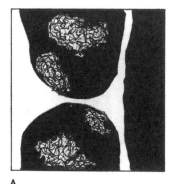

A

B

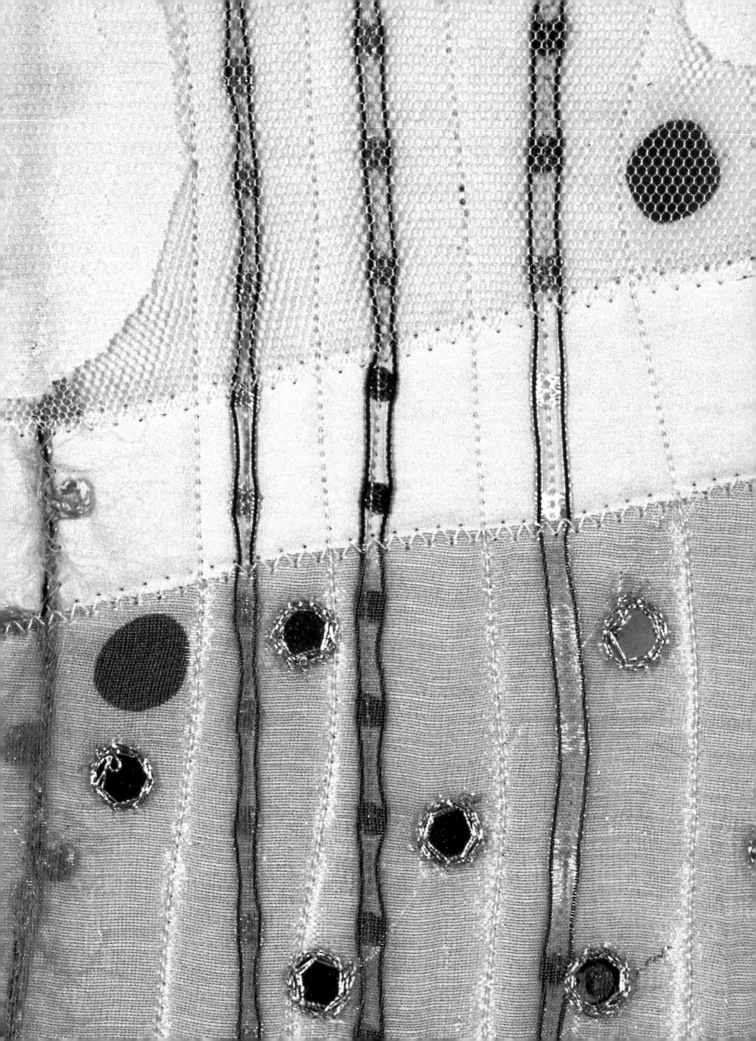

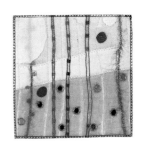

For this quilt I selected funky strips of yarn, covered them with sheer fabrics, and stitched them together. The yarn lines add a nice design element in addition to texture and a tip-of-the-hat to another craft.

Funky Yarn, Sheer Fabric

MATERIALS

White cotton fabric
(two 10" x 10" [25 x 25cm] pieces)

Quilt batting
(one 10" x 10" [25 x 25cm] piece)

Five 7½" (18.7cm) pieces of funky yarn, each different

Two 7" x 4" (17.5 x 10cm) pieces of sheer fabrics

White thread

Black thread

6" x 6" (15 x 15cm) template

INSTRUCTIONS

1. Prepare your quilt by making a sandwich of the top white cotton fabric, the quilt batting, and the bottom white fabric.

2. Randomly lay each of the five pieces of yarn vertically on the quilt top. Stitch them in place using white thread. Thick yarn can be stitched by sewing right over it using a straight stitch. Thin yarn should be stitched by sewing with a zigzag stitch. **(A)**

3. Place the two 7" x 4" (17.5 x 10cm) pieces of sheer fabric horizontally about 1" (2.5cm) apart, but with a slight slant upward on the quilt. The yarn will not be totally covered by the two sheer fabrics. Using a zigzag stitch, sew over the raw fabric edges, attaching them to the quilt. **(B)**

4. Using a straight stitch, sew straight white lines vertically between the yarn sections. If your sheer fabrics have patterns on them, follow the patterns when sewing. **(C)**

5. Place the 6" x 6" (15 x 15cm) template on the quilt top to find the desired angle and placement of design.

6. To cut the quilt to size and finish the edges, refer to the "Finishing the Quilts" instructions in the "Getting Started" section on page 19. Use black thread when sewing straight and zigzag stitches.

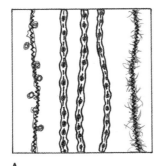

A

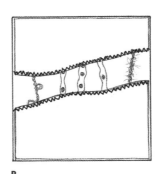

B

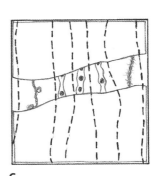

C

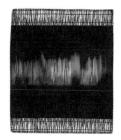

June 2004, 6" x 7" (15 x 17.5 cm)

The photo of my son graduating from high school was a big blur. At first I was quite unhappy about it, but I realized that I had been thinking about his graduation day for many years, and the whole day felt like a blur to me as well.

Graduation Day Blur

MATERIALS

White cotton fabric
(two 10" x 11" [25 x 27.5 cm] pieces)

Quilt batting
(one 10" x 11" [25 x 27.5 cm] piece)

One digital photo
(7" x 5" [17.5 x 12.5cm] shown)

One sheet of T-shirt
transfer paper

Black thread

Colored thread to
coordinate with photo

6" x 7" (15 x 17.5cm) template

INSTRUCTIONS

1. Choose a digital photo. Size it so that it will fit on the quilt. *Note: The photo must be printed reversed on the transfer paper, so that when ironed, it will be correct. Otherwise it will print backwards.* Follow the instructions on the transfer paper package; print the photo on T-shirt transfer paper. With the heat setting adjusted to the proper temperature for your transfer paper (refer to the instructions packaged with the item), iron transfer paper on fabric that will be used for the quilt top.

2. Prepare your quilt by making a sandwich of the photo-transferred fabric as the quilt top fabric, the quilt batting and the bottom white fabric. **(A)**

3. Sew straight lines on the quilt over the photo using black thread or other colors that coordinate with the photo. If you don't know where to stitch the lines, sew large zigzag lines across the photo or the edge of the photo as decoration. **(B)**

4. Place the 6" x 7" (15 x 17.5cm) template on the quilt top to find the desired angle and placement of design.

5. To cut the quilt to size and finish the edges, refer to the "Finishing the Quilts" instructions in the "Getting Started" section on page 19. Use black thread when sewing straight and zigzag stitches.

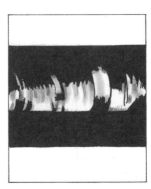

A

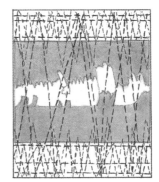

B

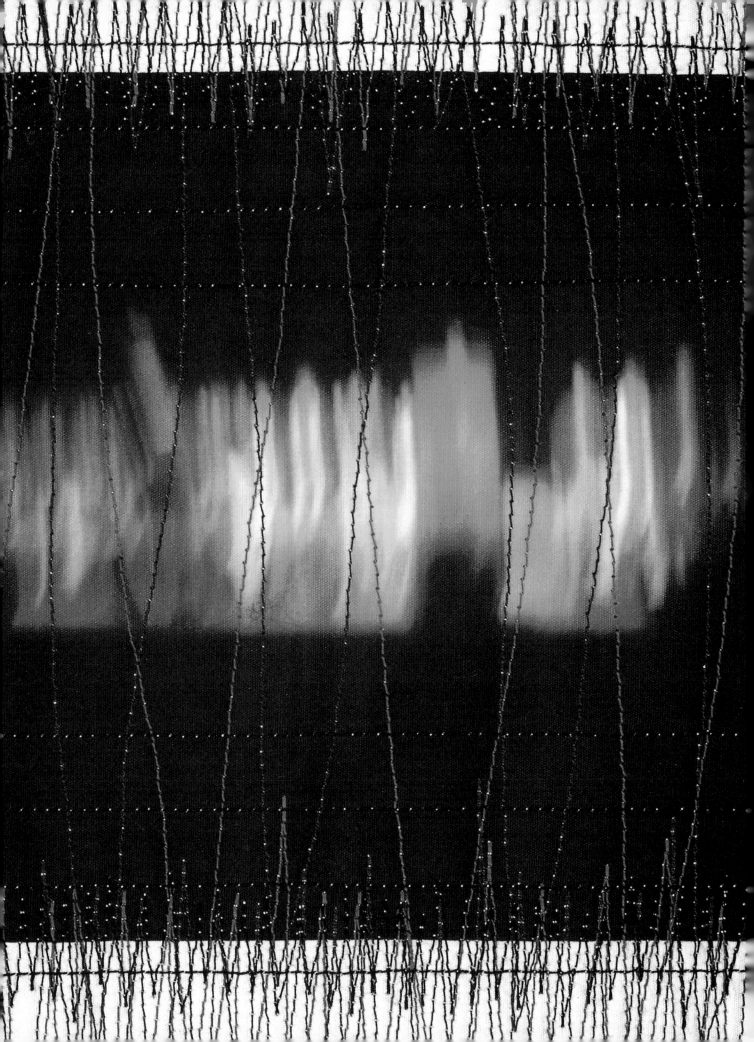

Inspired by the heated debate of the 2004 presidential elections, and with the red and blue states foremost on my mind, I made this quilt with strips of fabric woven and then quilted.

Red & Blue States

MATERIALS

White cotton fabric
(two 10" x 11" [25 x 27.5cm] pieces)

Quilt batting
(one 10" x 11" [25 x 27.5cm] piece)

Nine ½"–¾" (1.2–1.8cm)-wide
x 8" (20cm)-long strips of blue
patterned fabric

Nine ½"–¾" (1.2–1.8cm)-wide
x 8"-long strips of red patterned
fabric

Red thread

Blue thread

Black thread

6" x 7" (15 x 17.5cm) template

INSTRUCTIONS

1. Prepare your quilt by making a sandwich of the top white cotton fabric, the quilt batting, and the bottom white fabric.

2. Lay the nine strips of blue fabric vertically on the quilt top. Weave the red strips of fabric though the blue strips, going over one, under the next, and so on. Pin in place, if necessary. **(A)**

3. Alternating red and blue thread, stitch wavy lines across the quilt. Stitch from side to side to give the impression of a flag waving. **(B)**

4. Place the 6" x 7" (15 x 17.5cm) template on the quilt top to find the desired angle and placement of design (slight rotation shown on quilt).

5. To cut the quilt to size and finish the edges, refer to the "Finishing the Quilts" instructions in the "Getting Started" section on page 19. Use black thread when sewing straight and zigzag stitches.

A

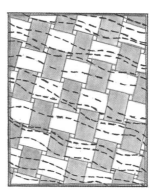

B

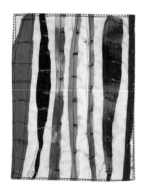

September 2005, 6" x 8" (15 x 20cm)

The scene: Saturday night at 11:45 pm. The mood: rushing to sew a quilt for the week. I quickly stitched together scraps of dyed silk scarves before my self-imposed midnight deadline.

Late Night Result

MATERIALS

White cotton fabric (two 10" x 12" [25 x 30cm] pieces)

Quilt batting (one 10" x 12" [25 x 30cm] piece)

Seven 9"-long strips of scrap fabric, varying widths ¼" (.6cm) to 1" (2.5cm) (scraps of dyed silk scarves shown)

Black thread

6" x 8" (15 x 20cm) template

INSTRUCTIONS

1. Prepare your quilt by making a sandwich of the top white cotton fabric, the quilt batting, and the bottom white fabric.

2. Cut seven 9" (22.5cm)-long strips of scrap fabric, varying widths ¼" (.6cm) to 1" (2.5cm). Misshapen strips will add to the charm of the quilt.

3. Lay the pieces of scrap fabric on the quilt top vertically, leaving a minimum of ¼" (.6cm) between each piece. **(A)**

4. Stitch the strips of fabric to the quilt with black straight stitches. Thinner strips require only one stitched line. Wider stitches will require stitching near both edges of the strips. **(B)**

5. Place the 6" x 8" (15 x 20cm) template on the quilt top to find the desired angle and placement of design.

6. To cut the quilt to size and finish the edges, refer to the "Finishing the Quilts" instructions in the "Getting Started" section on page 19. Use black thread when sewing straight and zigzag stitches.

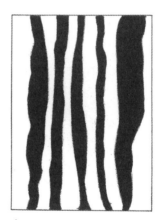

A

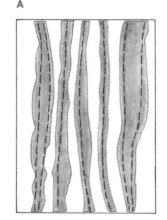

B

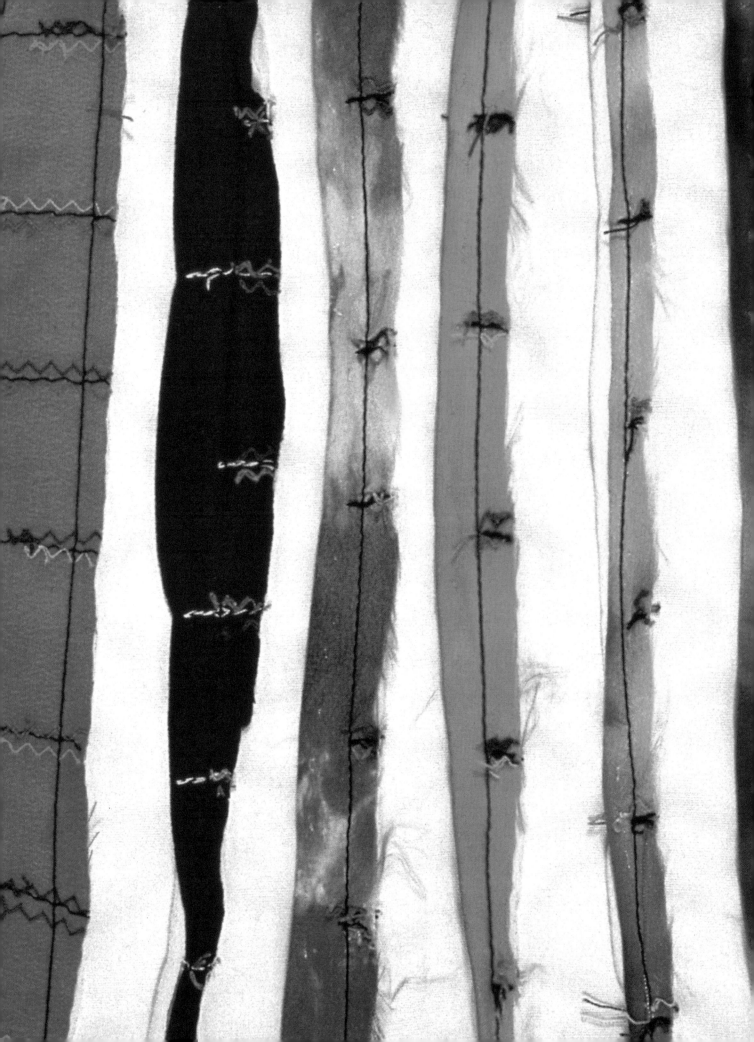

To make this simple graphic quilt, I combined ribbons from two holiday packages and two pieces of black paper from a box of chocolates.

Chocolates & Ribbon

MATERIALS

White cotton fabric
(two 10" x 12" [25 x 30cm] pieces)

Quilt batting
(one 10" x 12" [25 x 30cm] piece)

One 1½" (3.7cm)-wide pink ribbon, 7" (17.5cm) long

One ⅜" (.9cm)-wide red ribbon, 9" (22.5cm) long

Two 3½" x 3½" (8.75 x 8.75cm) pieces of black paper, textured if possible

White thread

Black thread

6" x 8" (15 x 20cm) template

INSTRUCTIONS

1. Prepare your quilt by making a sandwich of the top white cotton fabric, the quilt batting, and the bottom white fabric.

2. Place the pink ribbon horizontally on the quilt top. (If the ribbon has writing on it, turn it upside down so the writing is not easily readable.) Stitch near the edges using white thread.

3. Place the red ribbon vertically on the quilt top, over the pink ribbon. Stitch near edges using white thread.

4. Cut two 3½" x 3½" (8.75 x 8.75cm) pieces of black paper, textured if possible.

5. Sew one piece of black paper in the lower right corner of the quilt—¼" (.6cm) away from the sewn ribbons—using white straight stitches.

6. Sew the second piece of black paper in the upper left corner of the quilt—¼" (.6cm) away from the sewn ribbons—using white straight stitches.

7. Place the 6" x 8" (15 x 20cm) template on the quilt top to find the desired angle and placement of design.

8. To cut the quilt to size and finish the edges, refer to the "Finishing the Quilts" instructions in the "Getting Started" section on page 19. Use black thread when sewing straight and zigzag stitches.

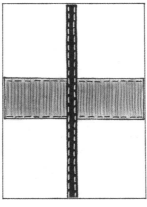

A

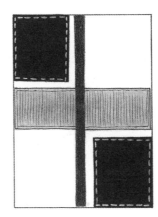

B

November 2003, 6" x 6" (15 x 15cm)

Before knitting a few scarves for winter, I knit a few thin sample strips to test the yarns. The texture of knitted yarn is very different from the woven fabric texture commonly seen on quilts.

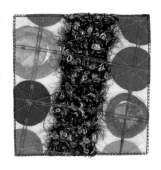

Knit-Sample Collage

MATERIALS

White cotton fabric
(two 10" x 10" [25 x 25cm] pieces)

Quilt batting
(one 10" x 10" [25 x 25cm] piece)

One 2" (5cm)-wide and 7½"-(18.7cm) long knitted strip (or substitute a piece of old sweater)

Eight 2" (5cm)-wide fabric circles (in assorted colors that coordinate with the knitted strip)

Six 7½" (18.7cm)-long strips of funky yarn

White thread

Black thread

6" x 6" (15 x 15cm) template

INSTRUCTIONS

1. Prepare your quilt by making a sandwich of the top white cotton fabric, the quilt batting, and the bottom white fabric.

2. Prepare one 2" (5cm)-wide and 7½"-(18.7cm)-long knitted strip (substitute a piece of old sweater). Place the knitted strip vertically on the quilt top, and stitch the edges with straight white stitches.

3. Place the 2" (5cm)-wide fabric circles vertically on the quilt top, ¼" (.6cm) from both sides of the knitted strip. Pin the circles to the quilt. **(A)**

4. Place the six 7½" (18.7cm) strips of yarn over the circles and knitted strip, creating a grid pattern.

5. Using white thread, sew over the yarn using straight stitches. (If the yarn is thin, stitch zigzag stitches over the yarn.) Stitch straight decorative lines on the quilt. **(B)**

6. Place the 6" x 6" (15 x 15cm) template on the quilt top to find the desired angle and placement of design. Pivot template counter clockwise slightly to achieve the look shown.

7. To cut the quilt to size and finish the edges, refer to the "Finishing the Quilts" instructions in the "Getting Started" section on page 19. Use black thread when sewing straight and zigzag stitches.

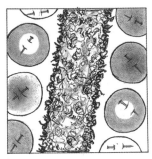

A

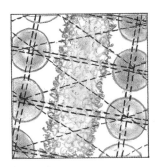

B

Resources

You may find many of the materials you need to make the projects in this book by looking through your junk and craft drawers. If you don't have what you need on hand, a trip to your local arts and craft store, office supply chain, or fabric store will get you ready to begin. Using the list below, you can go to a company's website to locate the store nearest you, order online, or place an order over the phone.

Basic Supplies

Cotton fabric–419W Bleached, Mercerized Combed Broadcloth 60" (152.4cm) wide, available at Testfabrics Inc., 570-603-0432, www.testfabrics.com

Warm & Natural Cotton Batting available at Joann stores, www.joann.com

Gutermann Thread available at SoloSlide Fasteners, 800-547-4775, www.soloslide.com

Straight pins available at SoloSlide Fasteners, 800-547-4775, www.soloslide.com

Scissors available at Staples, 800-378-2753, www.staples.comUsed sewing machines can be found at www.craigslist.org or www.ebay.com

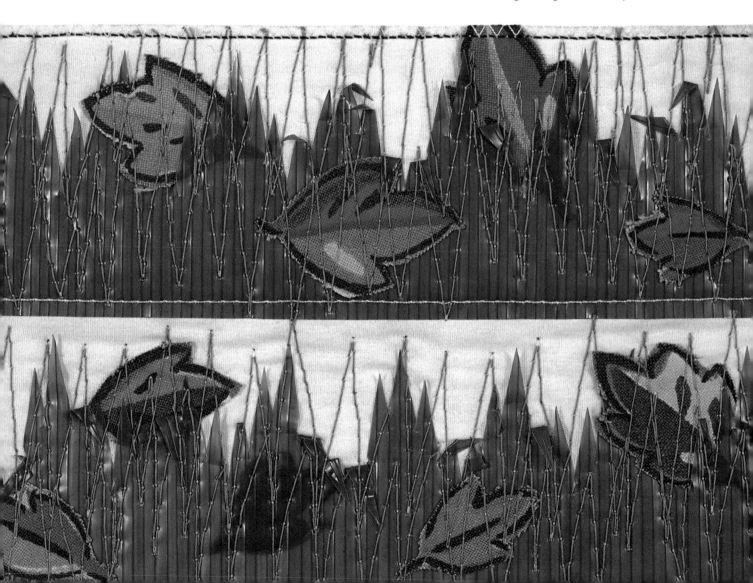

Iron available at Bed Bath and Beyond, 800-462-3966 or www.bedbathand beyond.com, or look for used irons at www.craigslist.org or www.ebay.com

Ironing board available at Bed Bath and Beyond, 800-462-3966 or www. bedbathandbeyond.com, or look for used irons at www.craigslist.org or www.ebay.com

Laundry pens or nonwashable markers available at Joann stores, www.joann.com

X-Acto Light-Duty Knife, #11 Blade, available at Staples, 800-378-2753, www.staples.com

Plastic Supplies

Yarn available at available at A. C. Moore, www.acmoore.com

Clementine boxes with red netting available at your local market, when in season

Onion netting bags available at your local market

Nonskid rug padding available at Bed Bath and Beyond, 800-462-3966 or www.bedbathandbeyond.com

Ribbon available at Joann stores, www.joann.com

Plastic sushi grass available at Sushi Foods Company, 888-817-8744, www.sushifoods.com

Orange construction fence available at U.S. Fence, 800-455-5167, www.us-fence.com

Crayola Large Size Crayons available at Dick Blick Art Materials, 800-828-4548, www.dickblick.com

Jacquard Textile Colors Fabric paint available at Dharma Trading Co. 800-542-5227, www.dharmatrading.com

Paper Supplies

Fabric netting available at Joann stores, www.joann.com

Paper shredder available at Staples, 800-378-2753, www.staples.com

Ribbon available at Joann stores, www.joann.com

Mailing seals available at Staples, 800-378-2753, www.staples.com

Cupcake wrappers available at your local market

Wrapping paper available at The Container Store, 888-266-8246, www.containerstore.com

Landscape fabric available at www.amazon.com

Paper available at Paper.com, 203-652-2500, www.paper.com

Paper maps available at AAA, www.aaa.com

Decorative pocket tissues available at www.platesandnapkins.com

Card stock available at Staples, 800-378-2753, www.staples.com

Rotary paper trimmers available at Staples, 800-378-2753, www.staples.com

Surface Design Supplies

Jacquard Textile Colors fabric paint available at Dharma Trading Co., 800-542-5227, www.dharmatrading.com

Neopaque (Opaque) fabric paint available at Dharma Trading Co., 800-542-5227, or www.dharmatrading.com

Lumiere (metallic) fabric paint available at Dharma Trading Co., 800-542-5227, or www.dharmatrading.com

Laundry pens or nonwashable markers available at Joann stores, www.joann.com

1" x 1" x 2" Art Gum Eraser available at Dick Blick Art Materials, 800-828-4548, www.dickblick.com

1" x 1" x 1" Art Gum Eraser available at Dick Blick Art Materials, 800-828-4548, www.dickblick.com

X-Acto Light-Duty Knife, #11 Blade, available at Staples, 800-378-2753, www.staples.com

Silklike plants available at A. C. Moore, www.acmoore.com

Crayola Large Size Crayons available at Dick Blick Art Materials, 800-828-4548, www.dickblick.com

White glue available at Staples,
800-378-2753, www.staples.com

Snow peas available at your
local market

Fabric net available at Joann stores,
www.joann.com

Lace available at Joann stores,
www.joann.com

Orange construction fence
available at U.S. Fence, 800-455-5167,
www.us-fence.com

Fiber Supplies

Storm Queen Felt Weather
Stripping available at DoItYourself.com,
866-835-5643, www.doityourself.com

Silklike leaves available at Joann stores,
www.joann.com

Fabric net available at Joann stores,
www.joann.com

Jacquard Textile Colors fabric paint
available at Dharma Trading Co.,
800-542-5227, www.dharmatrading.com

Silklike flowers with leaves available at
A. C. Moore, www.acmoore.com

Woven clothing labels available at
Name Maker, 800-241-2890,
www.namemaker.com

Fabric measuring tape available
at Joann stores, www.joann.com

Yarn available at A. C. Moore,
www.acmoore.com

Garden (or bird) netting available at
Gardeners Supply Company,
888-833-1412, www.gardeners.com

T-shirt transfer paper available at
Staples, 800-378-2753, www.staples.com

Ribbon available at Joann stores, www.
joann.com

Textured papers available at Paper.com,
203-652-2500, www.paper.com

Index

Note: Page numbers followed by f indicate figures.